FLOYD CLYMER'S MOTORCYCLIST'S LIBRARY

The Book of the
SUNBEAM S7 and S8

A PRACTICAL GUIDE FOR OWNERS
OF SUNBEAM MOTOR-CYCLES
(COVERS ALL 500 C.C. O.H.C.
VERTICAL TWINS FROM 1946
TO 1957)

BY

W. C. HAYCRAFT
F.R.S.A.

ANNOUNCEMENT

By special arrangement with the original publishers of this book, Sir Isaac Pitman & Son, Ltd., of London, England, we have secured the exclusive publishing rights for this book, as well as all others in THE MOTORCYCLIST'S LIBRARY.

Included in THE MOTORCYCLIST'S LIBRARY are complete instruction manuals covering the care and operation of respective motorcycles and engines; valuable data on speed tuning, and thrilling accounts of motorcycle race events. See listing of available titles elsewhere in this edition.

We consider it a privilege to be able to offer so many fine titles to our customers.

FLOYD CLYMER
Publisher of Books Pertaining to Automobiles and Motorcycles

2125 W. PICO ST.   LOS ANGELES 6, CALIF.

INTRODUCTION

Welcome to the world of digital publishing ~ the book you now hold in your hand, while unchanged from the original edition, was printed using the latest state of the art digital technology. The advent of print-on-demand has forever changed the publishing process, never has information been so accessible and it is our hope that this book serves your informational needs for years to come. If this is your first exposure to digital publishing, we hope that you are pleased with the results. Many more titles of interest to the classic automobile and motorcycle enthusiast, collector and restorer are available via our website at www.VelocePress.com. We hope that you find this title as interesting as we do.

NOTE FROM THE PUBLISHER

The information presented is true and complete to the best of our knowledge. All recommendations are made without any guarantees on the part of the author or the publisher, who also disclaim all liability incurred with the use of this information.

TRADEMARKS

We recognize that some words, model names and designations, for example, mentioned herein are the property of the trademark holder. We use them for identification purposes only. This is not an official publication.

INFORMATION ON THE USE OF THIS PUBLICATION

This manual is an invaluable resource for the classic motorcycle enthusiast and a "must have" for owners interested in performing their own maintenance. However, in today's information age we are constantly subject to changes in common practice, new technology, availability of improved materials and increased awareness of chemical toxicity. As such, it is advised that the user consult with an experienced professional prior to undertaking any procedure described herein. While every care has been taken to ensure correctness of information, it is obviously not possible to guarantee complete freedom from errors or omissions or to accept liability arising from such errors or omissions. Therefore, any individual that uses the information contained within, or elects to perform or participate in do-it-yourself repairs or modifications acknowledges that there is a risk factor involved and that the publisher or its associates cannot be held responsible for personal injury or property damage resulting from the use of the information or the outcome of such procedures.

WARNING!

One final word of advice, this publication is intended to be used as a reference guide, and when in doubt the reader should consult with a qualified technician.

PREFACE

FEW modern luxury-type motor-cycles have made such a well-merited and rapid climb to widespread popularity as the sleek-looking 487 c.c. overhead-camshaft vertical twin Sunbeam, officially introduced to the public (as Model S7) on 21st December, 1946.

Designed by a very talented engineer, Mr. E. Poppe, and manufactured by Sunbeam Motor Cycles, Ltd., Armoury Road, Birmingham 11 (with the vast B.S.A. resources behind them), the vertical twin Sunbeam veritably bristles with ingenious and worth-while features. From stem to stern it has been designed *as a whole*, and has no unsightly or incompatible "attachments." The net result is a "civilized motor-cycle" (the aim and claim of its designer) of almost enchanting appearance, with a remarkably smooth and lively performance, genuine mechanical silence, and exceptionally good reliability; a machine which neither discomforts nor dirties the rider, nor calls upon him to devote excessive spare time to maintenance.

Some regular and correct maintenance attention, however, is essential to the efficient running of even the best motor-cycles, and the main purpose of this handbook is to provide in a readable and non-technical form those essential maintenance instructions which, if conscientiously observed, will enable you to cruise on your Sunbeam in the sunshine for the maximum trouble-free miles at minimum expense and with maximum pleasure. Overhauling is also covered.

Many excellent detail modifications have been made to the vertical twin Sunbeam since its original introduction in 1946, although the design has remained basically unchanged. To prevent any confusion being caused on account of the modifications, the author has clearly dated instructions where these apply only to machines manufactured during a particular period. Where instructions are not dated, these may be regarded as applicable to all 1946 and later type Sunbeams.

Full maintenance instructions are given for the following models—

1. The 1946–9 Model S7 (Sunbeam forks).
2. The 1949–57 Model S8 (B.S.A. type front forks).
3. The 1949–57 Model S7 de luxe (B.S.A. type front forks).

The author thanks Mr. D. W. Munro of the Sunbeam Technical Department for kindly supplying much valuable technical data

PREFACE

and for permitting many Sunbeam copyright illustrations to be reproduced. The various accessory firms too have been most helpful, and the author thanks the Editor of *Motor Cycle* for kindly according permission to reproduce some excellent "exploded" views of the Sunbeam engine and gearbox unit.

W. C. H.

CONTENTS

CHAP.		PAGE
I.	HANDLING A SUNBEAM	1
II.	CORRECT CARBURATION	17
III.	SUNBEAM LUBRICATION	29
IV.	CARE OF THE LIGHTING SYSTEM	41
V.	GENERAL MAINTENANCE AND OVERHAUL	53
	Index	117

CHAPTER I

HANDLING A SUNBEAM

You are assumed to be the proud rider of a one-owner 487 c.c. Model S7 de luxe or Model S8 overhead-camshaft vertical twin Sunbeam, magnificent in its mist-green, silver grey, or black lustre finish, or else to have been lucky enough to purchase in sound condition at a reasonable price a second-hand Model S7, S7 de luxe, or Model S8. In either case you possess a machine which delights the eye, is easy to handle, and is a revelation to ride.

If you have had previous motor-cycling experience, you should experience no difficulty in getting on the road forthwith. If you are a complete novice you need also harbour no fears about quickly mastering your Sunbeam. Its controls are very simple, starting is extremely easy, and the machine is very stable, flexible, and responsive. Indeed, thanks largely to shaft drive and a twin-cylinder engine, one can ride a Sunbeam at a mere crawl without experiencing any transmission snatch or vibration (often present with singles).

For many reasons the Sunbeam quickly inspires confidence in the veriest novice. If you come within this category, the author assumes that you have at least an elementary knowledge of motor-cycles, are aware of the principles of the four-stroke engine, the reasons for the various controls, and have perused a copy of the "Highway Code."

For the benefit of the novice a summary of vital preliminaries may prove helpful. Most of them can generally be attended to by the dealer from whom the machine is purchased.

Getting on the Highway. You are not allowed by law to ride a motor-cycle on the public highway until you have attended to the preliminaries enumerated below. You must—

1. Take out an insurance policy to cover all third-party risks (personal injuries), and obtain the vital "certificate of insurance." With a new machine obtain a "cover note" pending the issue of the actual policy and certificate. It is advisable to insure a valuable Sunbeam against fire, theft, and damage, and you would be well advised to take out full comprehensive insurance.

2. Obtain a registration licence and registration book (Form R.F.1/2), or renew your licence (Form R.F.1/A), whichever is

applicable. When obtaining a new licence you are required to state on the application form the engine and frame numbers of your machine. On all Sunbeams the engine number is stamped on a rectangular machined face at the front of the crankcase below the dynamo. The frame number is stamped on the nearside lug under the peak of the saddle just at the rear of the tank.

Fig. 1. A "Civilized" Motor-cycle—Exhaust-side View of the 487 c.c. O.H.C. Vertical Twin Model S8 Sunbeam (1949 onwards)

All Sunbeam models have unit construction of engine and gearbox; a bore and stroke of 2¾ in. × 2½ in.; a linered cylinder block; lead-bronze big-end bearings; a chain-driven overhead camshaft; car-type lubrication; Lucas coil ignition and lighting (with C.V.C.); shaft drive; rear springing, etc.

The annual tax payable for all Sunbeams is £3 15s. plus an additional tax of £1 5s. if a sidecar is fitted.

3. If you intend to carry a pillion rider, securely *fix* a proper pillion seat to the machine. Your passenger must sit *astride* the seat. Pillion footrests are essential, though the law does not insist that they be fitted. If you are a "learner," your pillion rider must hold a current annual driving licence.

4. If your Sunbeam is second-hand, satisfy yourself that the speedometer needle *is* registering speed accurately. The speedometer *must* indicate when 30 m.p.h. is being exceeded within 10 per cent accuracy (*see* also page 52).

5. Get a (six-monthly) "provisional" licence (for "learners"), or a (three-year) full driving licence (both Form D.L.1), according to which you are entitled to. See also page 16.

6. If not eligible for an annual driving licence (*see* page 3), fit "L" plates to the front and rear of the machine pending your

passing an official driving test (Form D.L.26). See that the "learner" plates do not obscure your index and registration numbers. Note carefully that you are not eligible for a (three-

Fig. 2. Three-quarter Front View of the 487 c.c. Model S7 Sunbeam (1946–9)

The 1949 and later Model S7 de luxe is similar to the Model S7 shown, but like Model S8 has B.S.A.-type front forks (slightly larger) and some minor differences

year) full driving licence unless you are 16 years of age and have complied with *one* of the following conditions—

(*a*) You have held a licence (other than a provisional or visitor's licence) authorizing the driving of vehicles of the class or description applied for within a period of ten years ending on the date of coming into force of the licence applied for.

(*b*) You have passed the prescribed driving test (this includes a test passed while serving in H.M. Forces) during the said period of ten years.

A money-order post office supplies the Form needed.

A Useful Book for Sunbeam Owners. A book written by the author and likely to interest Sunbeam riders, especially beginners, is *The Art of Motor-cycling* (published by Pitman at 5s.). Its 127 pages and 75 illustrations cover comprehensively insurance, licensing, accessories, riding comfort, roadworthiness, sidecars, clothing, shields, learning to ride, engine principles, motor-cycle controls and their efficient use, changing gear, the technique of riding, numerous legal matters, the official driving test, road organizations, touring at home and abroad, etc.

THE SUNBEAM CONTROLS

"Clean" type handlebars (adjustable for angle) are a characteristic of all the vertical twin Sunbeams. As may be seen in Figs. 4 and

Fig. 3. The Attractive de luxe Tourer Model S 22/50 Sidecar for Models S7, S7 de luxe, and S8 Sunbeams

This single-seater Sunbeam design is well sprung, comfortable, and very roomy. It accommodates plenty of luggage, and has a close-fitting hood (shown down)

5, the number of controls on the handlebars has been reduced to the minimum, and the entire control layout is conveniently arranged so that the controls come readily to hand. For the benefit of the novice the author will now consider the disposition of the controls individually.

Petrol Taps. Two petrol taps and a "T" piece are located under the rear of the tank (except on most 1946–7 Model S7 Sunbeams) so as to enable a reserve supply of fuel to be maintained. This reserve is fed to the carburettor only when the second petrol tap is turned on. On the 1946–7 S7 Sunbeams with only one petrol tap there is a drain plug on the near side of the tank, and this plug has the same thread as the petrol tap. A conversion can thus be made if desired.

Every Sunbeam petrol tap has one serrated knob and one

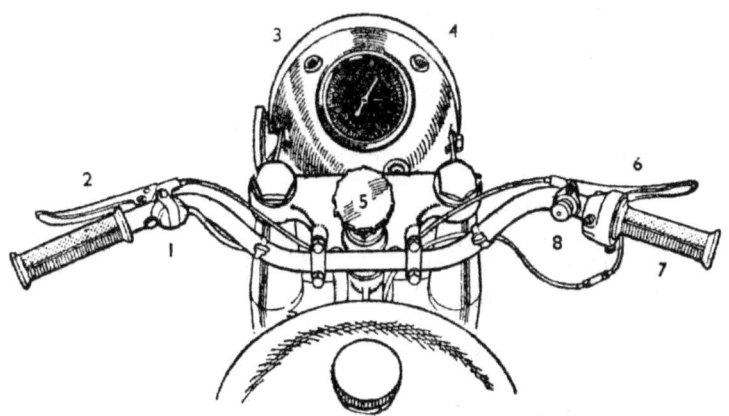

Fig. 4. Speedometer Mounting and Handlebar Control Layout on Models S7 de luxe and S8 (1949 onwards)

The "clean" handlebars are of B.S.A.-type and adjustable

1. Dip switch.
2. Clutch lever.
3. Ignition warning light (red).
4. Lubrication warning light (green).
5. Steering damper.
6. Front brake lever.
7. Throttle twist-grip
8. Horn button.

(*From "Motor Cycle," London*)

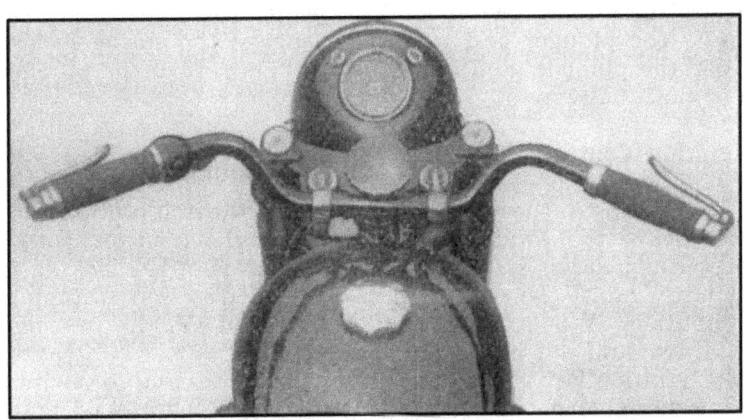

Fig. 5. Handlebar Control Layout on Model S7 (1946–9)

The "clean" handlebars are of Sunbeam design and on it (*left to right*) are the inverted clutch lever, twist-grip dip switch, horn button, throttle twist-grip, and inverted front brake lever

(*From "Motor Cycle," London*)

hexagonal knob. To turn on a petrol tap, push in the hexagonal knob; to turn it off, push in the serrated knob.

Throttle Twist-grip. The carburettor throttle slide controlling engine speed is operated by a rubber twist-grip on the off side of the handlebars. The total movement of the twist-grip is about a quarter of a turn. To open the throttle, turn the twist-grip *inwards* (i.e. anti-clockwise); to close the throttle, turn the twist-grip in the reverse direction.

A carburettor throttle stop (*see* Fig. 8) is provided to prevent the actual throttle slide closing completely. This enables the engine to tick-over when the throttle control is shut right back (with the ignition still switched on).

Strangler. No air lever is provided on the handlebars as is generally the case. Instead there is a strangler device for the carburettor choke, used only for *starting up the engine from cold*.

On 1946–9 Model S7 Sunbeams having no air filters the strangler consists of a lever situated immediately behind the bell on the carburettor air-intake. To operate the strangler, pull the lever to the *rear*.

On 1946–9 Model S7 Sunbeams with an air filter, and on all 1949 and subsequent Model S7 de luxe and S8 Sunbeams the strangler consists of a spring-loaded plunger (*see* Fig. 8) on the carburettor mixing chamber. To operate this type of strangler, depress the plunger and turn it to engage the spring lock. To release the plunger (and open the strangler), turn the plunger in the opposite direction.

Ignition Control. The only ignition control provided (and a very important one) is the ignition switch, which consists of a detachable key in the centre of the lighting switch (on the control panel below the saddle). To switch on the ignition, turn the ignition key *clockwise*. The ignition switch is of the locking type to guard against the risk of an unauthorized person switching on the ignition. When the ignition is switched off, the key can be withdrawn and put in a safe place.

The ignition key is used for starting purposes and for switching off (as no exhaust-valve lifter is provided). There is no ignition lever included on the handlebars because a centrifugal type automatic ignition advance mechanism (*see* Fig. 34) is provided in the combined distributor and contact-breaker unit.

Kick-starter Pedal. This is situated on the off side at the rear of the engine and gearbox unit, and its use is self-evident. Because of the fore and aft arrangement of the gear trains inside the gearbox, the kick-starter mechanism includes a right-angle skew gear drive. To prevent unnecessary wear of the skew gears, the kick-starter quadrant stop has (on 1946–7 Model S7) an external adjustment. This adjustment (*see* page 79) is most important.

Foot Gear-change Pedal. The foot gear-change pedal is conveniently disposed in relation to the off-side footrest and the spring-loaded lever has a slight downward inclination, to which position it is automatically returned after each gear change is effected. An indicator (*see* Fig. 6) is provided to indicate the four gear positions and "neutral" (which is between first and second gears). To change to a higher or lower gear, depress or raise the foot gear-change pedal, after disengaging the clutch.

Clutch Lever. The clutch lever is mounted on the near side of the handlebars. On the 1946–9 Model S7 Sunbeams an inverted-type clutch lever (*see* Fig. 5) is fitted, but all subsequent Sunbeams have an orthodox-type clutch lever as shown in Fig. 4. In either case, to disengage the clutch, pull the lever *towards* the handlebars.

It is necessary to disconnect the drive between the engine and rear wheel (by disengaging the clutch) immediately before making each gear change. When re-engaging the clutch after moving the gear-change pedal, always release the clutch lever gradually so as to ensure the drive being taken up smoothly and progressively. By so doing, you impose the minimum stresses on the engine, and transmission, and also reduce tyre wear.

Front Brake Lever. This control is similar to the clutch lever but is on the off side of the handlebars. To operate the front brake, pull the lever *towards* the handlebars. Note that it is not advisable to use the front brake alone. It is best used together with or slightly after the rear brake.

Rear Brake Pedal. The rear brake pedal is located on the near side, and the angle of the pedal in relation to the rider's foot is adjustable (*see* page 82) to suit individual requirements.

Lighting Switch and Ammeter. Both are mounted on a control panel built into the lid of the control box (located beneath the saddle), which contains the ignition coil and the compensated voltage control unit.

The lighting switch has three positions (Off, Low, and High) and these are explained on page 46. The dynamo charges in all three switch positions. The centre-zero ammeter, just behind the lighting switch, indicates the flow of current to and from the battery in amperes. Charge readings are shown on one side of the instrument, and discharge readings on the other side. For further information concerning the ammeter, *see* page 44.

Dip Switch and Horn Button. The dip switch controls the anti-dazzle filament of the headlamp double-filament main bulb and should always be used as an act of ordinary courtesy when about to pass an approaching vehicle at night. It should also be used instead of the horn between 11.30 p.m. and 7 a.m.

On 1946–9 Model S7 Sunbeams the dip switch comprises a twist-grip on the near side of the (Sunbeam-type) handlebars. To obtain a dipped beam, turn the twist-grip *inwards* (i.e. clockwise). On 1949 and subsequent S7 de luxe and S8 Sunbeams the dip switch consists of a normal-type small switch (*see* Fig. 4) mounted at the rear of the clutch lever on the near side of the (B.S.A.-type) handlebars.

Where a twist-grip dip switch is provided, the horn button is positioned close to the inner end of the near side twist-grip. If a small normal-type switch is fitted, the horn button is located on the off side of the handlebars close to the throttle twist-grip as shown in Fig. 4.

Warning Lights. Two warning lights (*see* Fig. 4) are incorporated in the headlamp shell so as to be readily observable by the rider. The green light on the right-hand side of the Smiths 120 m.p.h. speedometer is concerned with lubrication, and the red light on the other side with ignition. Both lights are observed when the ignition is switched on with the ignition key and the engine is stationary or ticking over at low r.p.m.

As soon as the oil pressure reaches a pre-determined figure, the green light goes out; it only shows again to warn the rider that oil pressure is low and the cause must be investigated. The red warning light goes out when the dynamo commences to charge the battery, and goes on again if the engine is stopped with the ignition left switched on. Do not leave the engine in this condition for long, because if the contacts of the contact-breaker happen to be closed, a continuous battery discharge may occur. Keep a watchful eye on both warning lights.

Steering Damper. All Sunbeam models have a steering damper (*see* Fig. 4) and it should be adjusted to suit road conditions and speed. When riding very fast over poor road surfaces, some tightening down of the damper steadies the steering which, however, is excellent without using the damper. Generally it is best to tighten down the damper gradually as the speed increases.

When slowing down to a low speed, be sure to slacken off the steering damper in good time, otherwise the machine may develop

HANDLING A SUNBEAM

a tendency to become unstable and lurch. On a sidecar outfit the damper can with advantage be kept slightly tightened down permanently while driving.

STARTING PROCEDURE

Before dealing with the subject of getting the engine started up, a few words concerning the Sunbeam stands may be of service to those with new mounts.

Operation of the Stands. All 1946-9 Model S7 Sunbeams have a central, easy-lift stand which can also be used as a prop stand if desired. To use the central stand as such, stand on the near side of the machine, press the stand downwards against the ground with the foot pushed against the pin on the near-side leg, and then gently draw the mount rearwards. It will readily roll up on to the central stand and when right back the stand automatically becomes locked with the rear wheel raised well clear of the ground.

To use the central stand as a prop stand only, press the stand downwards against the ground with the foot pushed against the pin on the near-side leg, and then release it. A ratchet will then hold the stand in this position.

To release the stand used either as a central stand or as a prop stand, depress the small pedal behind the near-side footrest so as to withdraw the ratchet, and simultaneously push the machine forward (if the machine has been raised clear of the ground). If the stand has been used for prop purposes only, you need merely touch the pedal to release the stand.

On all 1949 and subsequent Model S7 de luxe and S8 Sunbeams a central stand and a separate prop stand are provided. The central stand, however, has no ratchet and is therefore not self-locking. To operate this type of stand, use the method already described for the S7 central stand, disregarding the reference to the ratchet and pedal. The prop stand is fixed to the near side of the machine and folds against the frame tube. Its use is self-obvious.

Setting the Controls for Starting. To ensure a quick start, the following procedure is recommended—

1. Place the machine on its central stand (*see* previous paragraphs).
2. Verify that the foot gear-change pedal *is* in neutral (between first and second gears) by observing the gear-change indicator (*see* Fig. 6), or by noting whether it is possible to spin the rear wheel freely. When any of the four gears is engaged, turning the rear wheel also turns the engine and vice versa. If first gear

happens to be engaged, to obtain neutral, *depress* the foot gear-change very slightly until the feel of the pedal shows that neutral is selected.

3. Turn on the petrol tap, or one of the two taps (*see* page 4) by pushing in the hexagonal knob.

4. If the engine is quite cold, slightly flood the carburettor by momentarily depressing the tickler on the float chamber cover. If the engine is already warm, flooding is generally quite unnecessary.

5. Close the carburettor strangler (except when the engine is warm) by pulling the strangler lever to the rear or by depressing the spring-loaded plunger on the mixing chamber and turning it to lock it, according to the type of strangler control fitted (*see* page 6).

6. Open (inwards) the throttle twist-grip about one-tenth of a turn.

7. Switch on the ignition by turning the ignition key clockwise. Verify that the red warning light (*see* page 8) on the headlamp is illuminated as soon as the ignition is switched on.

Operating the Kick-starter. Having set the controls for starting as just described, all is now ready to start up the engine. Sitting astride the machine, or standing beside it, depress the kick-starter with the foot, using a deliberate but not too rough movement.

As automatic ignition advance mechanism is provided in the combined distributor and contact-breaker unit, you can safely apply a strong kick with the kick-starter without incurring any risk at all of a nasty kick-back resulting. The automatic advance mechanism, remember, automatically provides full retard for starting. In normal conditions the Sunbeam engine should fire at the first kick, but if the weather as well as the engine is cold, you may have to make a second attempt before the engine springs into life.

Open the Strangler Quickly. Within a few seconds of starting up from cold, you must open the strangler by pushing the starter lever forward or by releasing (by turning) the spring-loaded plunger on the mixing chamber, according to the type of strangler fitted (*see* page 6).

The strangler is designed specifically for starting purposes only, and it causes an excessively rich mixture to be sucked into the combustion chambers. If the strangler is not quickly opened, this excessively rich mixture may condense on the cylinder walls, dilute the vital oil film, produce heavy carbon deposits, and foul the sparking plug. A quite unnecessary wastage of fuel is also caused.

HANDLING A SUNBEAM

Warming Up the Engine. An excessively slow tick-over is bad, as this invites inadequate oil circulation when this is most needed, and induces a tendency to low-temperature condensation of fuel on, and corrosion of, the cylinder walls. An excessively fast warming up of the engine on the other hand is also bad, as this may cause internal friction until the oil is in proper circulation; it also causes overheating through lack of air cooling.

Always warm up the engine *moderately fast* for a minute or so before moving off. But never permit your Sunbeam power unit to idle too long. Note that, as previously mentioned, the ignition

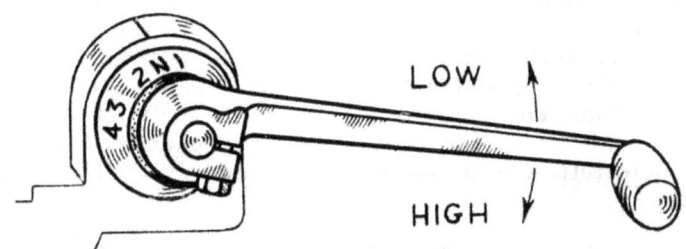

FIG. 6. THE FOOT GEAR-CHANGE INDICATOR

Although the pedal always returns to the same position, the indicator ring moves so that the gear numerals move into alignment with the stationary indicator mark, according to which gear is engaged

and lubrication warning lights should go out (*see* page 8) as soon as the dynamo starts to charge. Observe that they do so.

ON THE HIGHWAY

After warming up the engine, move the machine off its central stand with the gear-change lever in neutral, sit astride the saddle, and you are now ready to engage first (bottom) gear.

To Engage First Gear, disengage the clutch by pulling the clutch lever towards you to its full extent, and then *raise* the foot gear-change pedal fully with the toe until first gear is felt to engage. If you are in any doubt, look at the indicator (*see* Fig. 6). The gear-box internal dogs should immediately engage the respective gears, but if you experience any difficulty in engaging first gear, rock the motor-cycle backwards and forwards very slightly until perfect engagement is obtained. As soon as you engage first gear, remove the toe from the gear-change pedal, but keep the clutch lever fully disengaged.

Moving Off. Open the throttle slightly by turning the twist-grip inwards, and simultaneously release the clutch lever. You will then move off. As you gather speed and begin to accelerate, continue to increase the throttle opening progressively so as to prevent the engine stalling and maintain a steady acceleration of the engine and machine.

Changing Up (First to Second). If you are starting off on a downward gradient, you can change up from first to second (and the higher gears) immediately, but if you are starting off on the level, or particularly on an ascending gradient, you must throttle up the engine until the machine has plenty of momentum before making any attempt to change into second.

It is desirable to change into second gear when you have reached about 15 m.p.h. To do this, disengage the clutch, simultaneously close the throttle, pause a second, and then *depress* the foot gear-change pedal until second gear (*see* Fig. 6) is felt to engage. Then engage the clutch, immediately flick open the throttle, and remove the foot from the gear-change pedal, so as to allow it to return to its normal position ready for the next gear change.

Changing Up (to Third and Fourth). The required procedure is similar to that just described for changing up into second gear. Throttle up the engine until you are riding at about 25 m.p.h., disengage the clutch, simultaneously close the throttle, pause a second, and then gently *depress* the foot gear-change pedal fully until you feel that third gear is properly engaged (*see* Fig. 6). Then engage the clutch, quickly flick open the throttle, and remove the foot from the gear-change pedal.

To change up into fourth (top) gear, throttle up the engine until you attain a speed of 30–35 m.p.h., and then engage fourth gear, using the same procedure as for engaging third gear.

Changing Down (Fourth to Third). Changing down always involves a speeding up of the engine, and some riders prefer to leave the throttle open when each change into a lower gear is made by *raising* the foot gear-changing pedal. However, the following is the method most calculated to give a sweet and rapid downward change, free from unnecessary noise.

Throttle down the engine until you are running at a speed which is normal for third gear. Disengage the clutch, open the throttle slightly, pause a second, and then *raise* the foot gear-change pedal to its full extent with the toe until third gear is felt to engage. Now engage the clutch, remove the toe from the pedal, and simultaneously throttle up to allow for the considerable increase in the speed of the engine relative to that of the rear wheel.

On your S7 and S8 (not provided with a close-ratio racing

gearbox) avoid the considerable temptation to slam the gear-change pedal into third when you are approaching a corner and about 50 yards away. This causes over-revving of an engine not under power and if often indulged in causes much unnecessary wear and tear. If you feel that you must change down for a corner, wait until you actually reach it, and then snick in third gear neatly and in sufficient time to ensure a good get-away.

Changing Down (to Second and First). The changing procedure is similar to that just described for changing down from fourth to third gear. With the toe *raise* the foot gear-change pedal fully during each gear change. Each full movement of the pedal engages the next gear in the sequence shown by the indicator in Fig. 6.

When changing down, see that you do not do this at too high a road speed, because this may force the engine to turn over at excessively high revolutions per minute. Do not forget to rev up the engine during each gear change.

When making a change down from fourth or third gear to first (bottom) gear, it is not *essential*, except when hill climbing, to complete the full gear-changing procedure for each intermediate gear. You can reduce the speed of the machine to a crawl by closing the throttle and using both brakes, and then adopt the following procedure. Disengage the clutch and raise the foot gear-change pedal to its full extent twice or three times in quick succession, according to whether fourth or third gear was previously engaged. While making each change, "blip" or throttle up the engine slightly. The knack is soon mastered. Afterwards engage the clutch and throttle up the engine until you are travelling at a speed normal for first gear.

General Hints on Gear Changing. With the positive-stop foot gear-change provided on S7 and S8 Sunbeams, gear changing is extremely simple. With a little practice on a quiet road you will find that you can soon cover the full sequence of gear changing from first to top, or top to first, silently and smoothly in a few seconds. Here are some important gear-changing hints worth remembering—

1. Always change down *before* your engine shows signs of getting hot and bothered.

2. Make the best use of the four excellent gear ratios provided. The gear-change pedal always returns to the same position, but do not leave it there.

3. Never force your Sunbeam to climb a steep gradient unwillingly in top gear. This amounts to cruelty.

4. During each gear change, maintain a *light* pressure on the

foot gear-change pedal until the gear is felt to engage and the clutch lever is released. Remove the foot to the footrest at all other times.

5. When operating the clutch, throttle twist-grip, and gear-change pedal, employ a well co-ordinated and almost simultaneous movement, so that to onlookers the gear change is scarcely apparent.

6. Avoid racing the engine in the lower gears. This may sound good, but it is not as good as it sounds.

7. See that the gearbox does get its oil ration occasionally (*see* page 35).

Use of the Brakes. The brakes on the Sunbeam have large diameter drums and are very powerful. Rarely is it necessary to jam on both brakes hard. You should cultivate the habit of operating the front and rear brakes simultaneously when required, and drive as much as possible on the throttle, controlling speed by judicious use of the twist-grip.

When descending hills you can close the throttle, with a lower gear engaged, and make full use of engine compression as a brake. If the throttle-stop setting is such that the engine continues to fire, switch off the ignition temporarily.

Halting a Sunbeam. To make a normal halt (in neutral) on the road, operate the controls in the following manner—

1. Turn the twist-grip inwards until the throttle is completely closed.

2. Disengage the clutch.

3. Operate the front brake lever and the rear brake pedal together, increasing the hand and foot pressure as the brake linings contract on the brake drums.

4. Throttle up the engine slightly, and pause a second.

5. Raise the foot gear-change pedal fully until the next lower gear is felt to engage, and throttle up the engine after engaging the clutch. Repeat this procedure until first gear is obtained.

Alternatively raise the pedal two or three times in quick succession (*see* page 13) until the last (bottom) gear is engaged. Then *depress* the pedal very slightly to obtain neutral.

6. Release the clutch lever. The engine will now be ticking-over in neutral with the machine at a standstill.

7. If it is now desired to stop the engine, switch off the ignition by turning the ignition key anti-clockwise (see that the red warning light is out). If you intend to leave the machine standing for some length of time, for safety remove the detachable ignition key, and also turn off the petrol to prevent any accidental flooding of the carburettor.

Go Steady for 1,000 Miles. The normal running-in period for the Sunbeam O.H.C. vertical twin engine is 1,000 miles. If you want to spoil your engine quickly and permanently, do whatever you feel like during the vital running-in period.

On a brand new or reconditioned engine the bearing surfaces are a close running-fit and moreover are not dead smooth (they have tool marks not visible to the naked eye). Until these surfaces (and especially those of the cylinders and pistons) attain a mirror-like hardness and smoothness, excessive speed will necessarily generate excessive friction and heat, accompanied by inadequate lubrication, and such abuse is likely to ruin the surfaces once and for all.

Control yourself and your throttle twist-grip during the running-in period so that you never indulge in fierce bursts of speed. You will be rewarded a thousandfold, and after many thousands of miles the engine will retain its high power output and sweet running. After covering 1,000 miles you can step up the throttle openings gradually and progressively, but it is inadvisable to keep the machine on sustained full throttle until at least 1,500 miles have been covered. Incidentally, no motor-cycles except racing types should be kept on full throttle for prolonged periods. Below are some really important running-in hints—

1. Do not even momentarily turn the twist-grip throttle control fully inwards. Be content with cruising at 40–45 m.p.h. on main roads.

2. Avoid rapid acceleration, especially in the lower gears and when the machine is not under load.

3. Do not permit the engine to idle for long or at an excessive speed.

4. Make full use of the four-speed gearbox, and see that the engine never labours. Change down in good time and as often as is necessary to keep the engine running smoothly without an unduly large throttle opening.

5. Keep the engine, gearbox, and machine correctly lubricated (*see* Chapter III). Be particularly careful not to permit the level of oil in the engine sump to fall too low and thereby cause the reduced volume of oil in circulation to become too hot. Remember that a new engine runs hotter than one which has been run-in and there is therefore more heat to be dispersed.

If a Seizure Should Occur. In the unlikely and unhappy event of a partial or complete piston seizure occurring (rare unless running-in is neglected), instantly declutch and close the throttle. By doing this you will probably save considerable damage, and the only ill effect (which can be remedied) may be slight smearing of the lands between the piston rings. A seizure is indicated by the engine suddenly "pulling up" after hard driving.

After the First 250 Miles. With the appropriate spanners go over the various external nuts and bolts, especially those on the engine, and tighten any which may have slackened off. Check the tightness of the cylinder head nuts in the order shown in Fig. 61. Drain and replenish the oil sump with some fresh oil, and also clean the sump filter (*see* page 33). Repeat at 1,000 miles and subsequently about every 2,000 miles. During the initial life of an engine, oil contamination is somewhat greater than is the case later on. Check the contact-breaker gap after the first 500 miles (*see* page 64).

Upper Cylinder Lubricant Advised. During running-in the makers advocate the addition of some good quality upper cylinder lubricant to the petrol each time you replenish the fuel tank. Should upper cylinder lubricant not be available, you can add an eggcupful of engine oil to each two gallons of fuel. No harm can, of course, be done by continuing to use upper cylinder lubricant after the running-in period is completed, but this is not really necessary.

Long Term Driving Licences. Note that substantive driving licences lasting *three years* and costing 15s. are now obtainable by all riders who hold a "provisional" licence and satisfactorily complete their driving test. For most other riders a three-year driving licence has been available since 1st September, 1957, subject to the satisfactory completion of Form D.L.I. (*see* page 2, paragraphs 5, 6). Those with surnames beginning P–Z will have to wait until 1st September, 1959, before they can obtain a three-year licence instead of an annual licence.

CHAPTER II

CORRECT CARBURATION

ALL 487 c.c. overhead-camshaft vertical twin Sunbeams have an Amal needle-jet type carburettor specified. It is almost identical to the standard type needle-jet Amal instrument fitted to the majority of motor-cycles, but there is a slight difference.

On the 1946-9 Model S7 Sunbeams not provided with an air filter, the carburettor (type 276BO/3A) is a single-lever type, a strangler device (for starting up from cold) being incorporated on the carburettor air-intake. On the 1946-9 Model S7 Sunbeams with a Vokes air filter, and on all 1949 and subsequent Model S7 de luxe and S8 Sunbeams, the carburettor (type 276DO/3A) is a two-lever type; a separate air slide (used for starting up from cold) operates inside the throttle slide and constitutes the strangler (sometimes referred to as the choke). It has not, however, the usual cable-operated handlebar control lever, but instead is actuated by a spring-loaded plunger on the mixing chamber of the carburettor. Details of this arrangement are clearly shown in Fig. 8, and the method of operating both types of stranglers is referred to on page 6.

Right from the start, the author would emphasize that all Sunbeams are sent out from the Birmingham factory with the carburettor very carefully tuned, and you are not advised to interfere with the maker's setting without having a very good reason. Some minor adjustments are, however, permissible. Carburettor tuning is discussed in detail later in this chapter.

HOW THE CARBURETTOR WORKS

A few words concerning the functioning of the Amal needle-jet carburettor should prove of interest and be helpful if you have occasion to make any adjustment. On the Amal instrument the mixture at slow or idling speeds is controlled by a readily adjustable pilot jet, while at higher speeds the mixture is controlled by means of a needle attached to a throttle slide and working in a restriction jet.

The carburettor is for all practical purposes automatic, the strangler being closed only to facilitate starting from cold. At all other times it should be fully opened. The throttle slide is chromium plated to provide a hard wearing surface. The air slide (where fitted) of the strangler has its surface similarly treated, and as already mentioned, has a spring-loaded plunger control. The throttle slide is operated by a cable and the twist-grip on the offside of the handlebars.

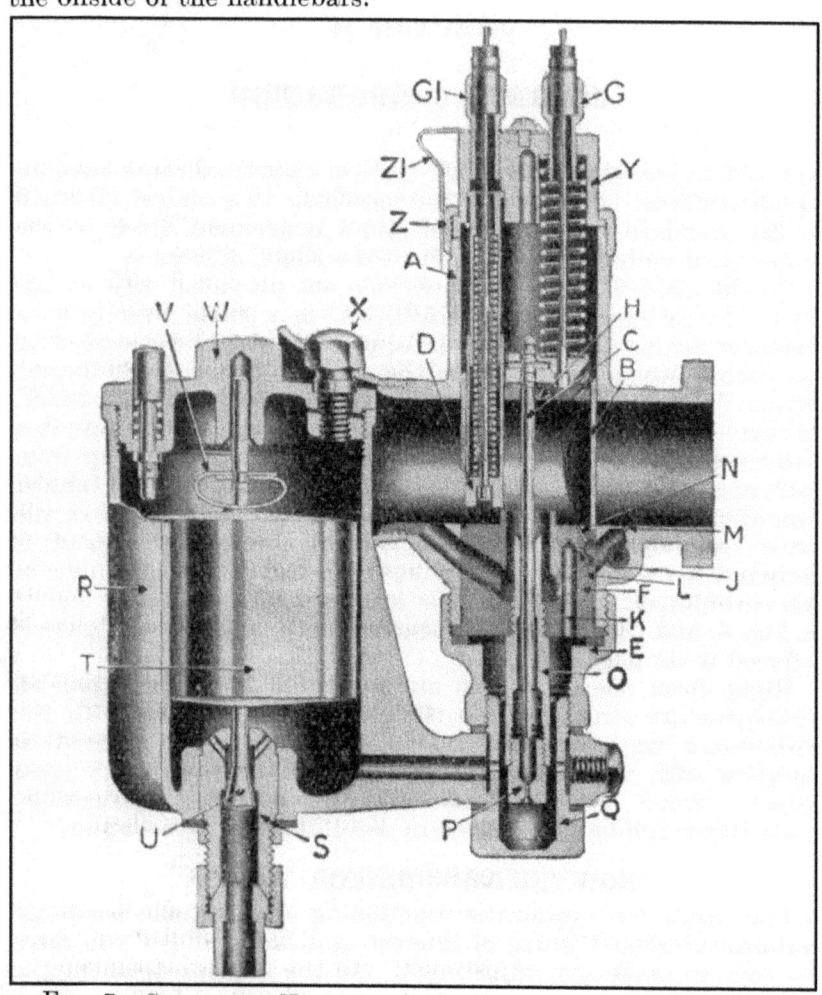

Fig. 7. Sectional View of Amal Needle-jet Carburettor

On Sunbeams where the strangler is not on the carburettor air-intake, control of the air slide *D* is by means of a spring-loaded plunger (*see* Fig. 8)

Referring to the sectional view (Fig. 7) illustrating the construction, *A* is the carburettor body or mixing chamber, the upper part of which has a throttle valve *B*, with taper needle *C* attached by the needle clip. The throttle valve regulates the quantity of mixture supplied to the engine. Passing through the

CORRECT CARBURATION 19

throttle valve is the air valve D of the strangler (where fitted), independently operated and serving the purpose of obstructing the main air passage for starting (*see also* Fig. 8). Fixed to the

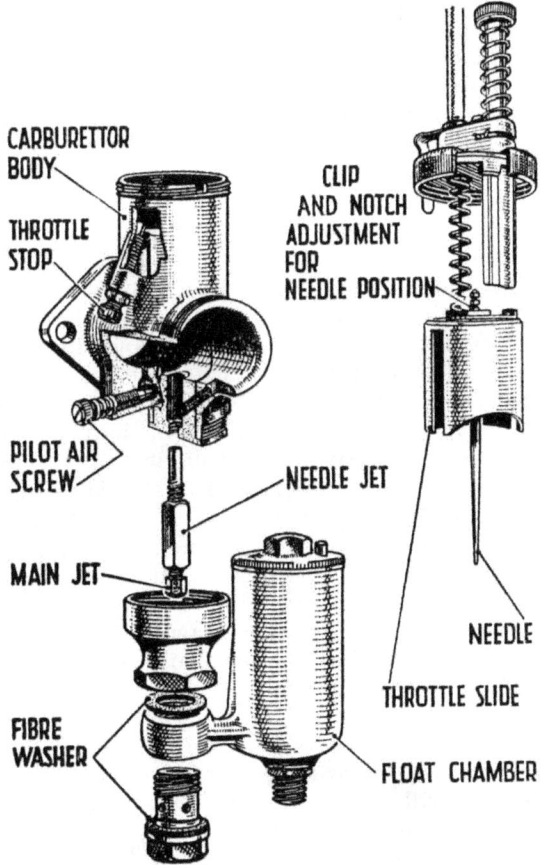

FIG. 8. EXPLODED VIEW OF AMAL NEEDLE-JET CARBURETTOR
On 1946–9 Model S7 Sunbeams without air filters the air slide and spring-loaded plunger control (*top right*) are omitted, the strangler being incorporated on the air-intake

underside of the mixing chamber by the union nut E is the jet block F, and interposed between them is a fibre washer to ensure a petrol-tight joint. On the upper part of the block is the jet block barrel H, forming a clean through-way. Integral with the jet block is the pilot jet J, supplied through the passage K. The adjustable pilot air intake L communicates with a chamber, from which issues the pilot outlet M and the by-pass N. A throttle stop (*see* Fig. 8) is provided on the mixing chamber, by which the position of the throttle valve for tick-over is regulated independently of the cable adjustment. The needle jet O is screwed in the underside of the jet block, and carries at its bottom end the main jet P. Both these jets are removable when the jet plug Q, which bolts the mixing chamber and the float chamber together, is removed. The float chamber, which has a bottom feed, consists of a cup R supplied with petrol through union S. It contains the float T and the needle valve U attached by the clip V. The float chamber cover W has a lock-screw X for security.

The petrol tap having been turned on, petrol will flow past the needle valve U until the quantity of petrol in the chamber R is sufficient to raise the float T, when the needle valve U will prevent a further supply entering the float chamber until some in the chamber has already been used up by the engine. The float chamber having filled to its correct level, the fuel passes along the passages through the diagonal holes in the jet plug Q, when it will be in communication with the main jet P and the pilot feed hole K; the level in the needle jet and pilot jet being, obviously, the same as that maintained in the float chamber.

Imagine the throttle valve B very slightly open. As the piston descends, a partial vacuum is created in the carburettor, causing a rush of air through the pilot air hole L and drawing fuel from the pilot jet J. The mixture of air and fuel is admitted to the engine through the pilot outlet M. The quantity of mixture capable of being passed by the pilot outlet M is insufficient to run the engine. This mixture also carries excess of fuel. Consequently, before a combustible mixture is admitted, throttle valve B must be slightly raised, admitting a further supply of air from the main air intake. The farther the throttle valve is opened, the less will be the depression on the outlet M, but, in turn, a higher depression will be created on the by-pass N, and the pilot mixture will flow from this passage as well as from the outlet M. The mixture supplied by the pilot and by-pass system is supplemented at about one-eighth throttle by fuel from the main jet P, the throttle valve cut-away determining the mixture strength from here to one-quarter throttle. Proceeding up the throttle range, mixture control by the needle position occurs from one-quarter to three-quarters throttle, and from this point the main jet is the only regulation.

The air valve D (where provided) has the effect of obstructing the main through-way and, in consequence, increasing the depression on the main jet, enriching the mixture. The throttle control cable has an adjuster at the handlebar end of the cable.

The Throttle-stop Screw. The throttle-stop adjusting screw (shown in Fig. 8) is normally adjusted so as to prop the throttle

CORRECT CARBURATION

slide open sufficiently to enable the engine to tick-over when the throttle twist-grip is completely closed.

The Pilot Air Adjusting Screw. This screw (*see* Fig. 8) controls the suction imposed on the pilot jet by altering the volume of air which mixes with the fuel. It controls the strength of the mixture for "idling" and also for initial throttle openings. To weaken the mixture the adjusting screw is screwed *outwards*.

The Main Jet. This regulates the fuel supply at throttle openings exceeding three-quarters full open. At smaller openings of the throttle, the fuel supplied passes through the main jet, but the amount is decreased due to the needle in the needle jet having a controlling effect. The main jet is screwed into the needle jet and can readily be detached after removing the jet plug shown at Q in Fig. 7. Referring to Fig. 8, to remove the main jet, hold the needle jet with one spanner, and with another unscrew the main jet.

Each Amal main jet is numbered and calibrated so that its precise discharge is known. It thus follows that any two main jets having the same number are identical in all respects. The larger the jet, the higher is its number. If a larger size jet is needed, on no account attempt to ream the existing jet, but obtain a new one of larger size.

The Needle and Needle Jet. The needle is attached to and moves with the throttle slide. Being tapered, it therefore permits more or less fuel to pass through the needle jet as the throttle is opened or closed respectively. This applies throughout the range of throttle openings, except at nearly full throttle and when "idling." The needle jet is of a specified size, and normally its size should not be changed.

As may be seen in Fig. 8, the position of the taper needle relative to the throttle opening can be adjusted according to the mixture required by securing the needle to the throttle with the needle spring clip in a particular groove, five of which are provided. Position No. 2, for example, means the second groove *from the top*. At throttle openings from one-quarter to three-quarters open, raising the needle enriches the mixture, while lowering the needle weakens it. Only one size of needle is available.

The Throttle Valve Cut-away. The throttle on the atmospheric side is cut away, and this affects the depression on the main fuel supply. The cut-away provides a means of tuning between the pilot and needle jet range of throttle opening. The actual amount of cut-away is denoted by a number marked on the throttle slide.

Thus 6/3 means a throttle type 6 with a No. 3 cut-away. A throttle with a larger cut-away (say, 6/5) weakens the mixture. Conversely, a smaller cut-away enriches the mixture.

TUNING THE CARBURETTOR

As previously stated, do not deviate from the maker's setting without good reason. Normally the only carburettor adjustment likely to be required is a pilot jet adjustment, which often has a marked effect on slow-running and easy starting. In certain circumstances it may be desirable to enrich the mixture by raising the needle one notch or by increasing the size of the main jet. To meet all contingencies, the author will describe carburettor tuning in detail.

Note the Exhaust. If carburation is correct, no trace of black smoke should be visible at the exhaust. Combustion is complete and carbon formation almost non-existent. Also where the mixture is right, the exhaust flame is of a *whitish-blue* colour.

If the mixture tends to be weak, the colour of the exhaust flame is *light blue*. If, on the other hand, the mixture is excessively rich, the flame is of a characteristic *yellow* colour, and some *black* smoke is generally present. Note that the above references to exhaust flames imply exhaust flames as observed at an *open* exhaust port.

If the Mixture is Weak. An excessively weak mixture is usually accompanied by (*a*) a generally sluggish engine, (*b*) some popping-back into the carburettor, (*c*) a tendency to overheat and "knock," (*d*) occasional misfiring, (*e*) bad slow-running, and (*f*) some hesitation in picking-up. A weak mixture, besides giving poor performance, is likely to burn the exhaust valve owing to slow combustion. Possible causes of a weak mixture are as follows—

1. Air leakage caused by a worn throttle slide or worn inlet valve guides.
2. Air leakage due to a poor joint at the flange fixing the carburettor to the manifold.
3. Incorrect tuning of the carburettor.
4. Badly adjusted or sticking throttle control.
5. A stoppage in the fuel pipe to the float chamber.
6. A sticking float chamber needle, or incorrect attachment of the float on the needle (rather unlikely).
7. A choked jet or filter.
8. Weak engine compression due to badly seating valves, or worn piston rings, worn cylinders, faulty cylinder head joint, etc.
9. An air lock in the fuel supply system.

It is fairly easy by a process of elimination to check whether a weak mixture is caused by a fault other than incorrect carburettor adjustment. For instance, engine compression can be tested by operating the kick-starter with the strangler wide open. Similarly, the state of the inlet valves can be determined by feeling whether they are slack in their guides. To check the fuel pipe, remove and blow through it. Normally it is unwise to meddle with the adjustment of the float chamber needle.

If the Mixture is Rich. An excessively rich mixture, though sometimes providing good power at high speeds, is generally accompanied by (*a*) black smoke at the exhaust, (*b*) sluggish running, (*c*) heavy fuel consumption, (*d*) a tendency for eight-stroking, (*e*) some misfiring at moderate and low speeds, (*f*) a tendency for the engine to choke, and (*g*) an engine which rapidly carbonizes, so causing a further decline in power output and an increasing tendency to "knock" under slight provocation. Possible causes for some or all of the above symptoms are enumerated below—

1. "Flooding" of the carburettor due to a punctured float, a bent or worn float needle, a defective needle seating, grit between the needle and the valve seating, or to too high a level of fuel in the jets.
2. A badly adjusted or sticking throttle control.
3. Incorrect carburettor tuning.

Flooding of the carburettor can be bad for the engine and must be rectified at once. But do not mistake real flooding for a leaky union below the float chamber, caused through insufficient tightening of the union nut. A leakage of this kind is apt to cause a weak mixture rather than an over-rich one.

Procedure for Tuning. Should the setting of the Amal carburettor not give entire satisfaction for particular requirements, there are four separate ways of rectifying matters as given herewith and the adjustments should be made in this order: (*a*) Main jet (three-quarters to full throttle); (*b*) pilot air adjustment (closed to one-eighth throttle); (*c*) throttle valve cut-away on the air intake side (one-eighth to one-quarter throttle); and (*d*) needle position (one-quarter to three-quarters throttle). The diagram (Fig. 9) clearly indicates the part of the throttle range over which each adjustment is effective.

The Amal carburettor is throughout the throttle range entirely automatic, and the air lever should be kept wide open, except for starting and until the engine has warmed up properly. It is assumed that normal petrol is used for tuning, which should be done in the sequence described below. Throttle openings to be used in the five tuning operations are those indicated in Fig. 9.

By closely following these tuning instructions (recommended by Amal, Ltd.) you will be assured of obtaining the most satisfactory performance with maximum economy of fuel. For tuning purposes it is advisable to get your Sunbeam started up on a quiet road having a slight up gradient, so as to impose a small load on the engine.

1. TO CHECK THE MAIN JET SIZE. Accelerate up to full throttle and carefully note the response of the engine to the twist-grip.

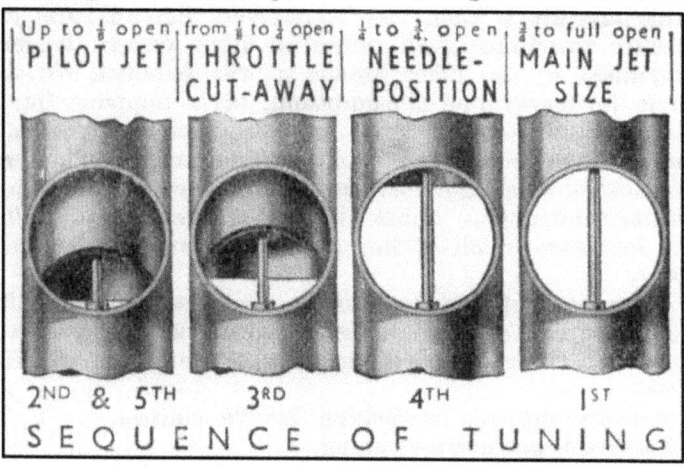

FIG. 9. TUNING SEQUENCE FOR AMAL CARBURETTOR

Should power output appear better with the throttle not completely open, this indicates that the main jet is too small, and the next larger size should be tried. Similarly, if there is a tendency for the engine to run "heavily" on full throttle, this denotes that the main jet is too large and the next smaller size should be experimented with.[1]

CARBURETTOR SETTING FOR 1946-57 SUNBEAMS

Carburettor	Main Jet	Needle Jet	Needle Position	Throttle Valve	Choke Size
276DO/3A	150	0·1075	2	6/3	15/16

If tuning for speed, be careful to choose a main jet of size sufficient to maintain the engine in a cool condition. Make a run

[1] Different size jets are obtainable from spares stockists, or from Amal, Ltd., Holdford Road, Witton, Birmingham 6.

at high speed, pull up, and stop the engine immediately. Remove the sparking plugs and closely inspect them. If the plugs are sooty, the mixture is too rich. Should the body of a plug be dry grey in colour, the mixture is on the weak side, and a larger size jet is required. With a properly proportioned mixture, the plug body should have a bright black appearance. Also, when running, observe the sound of the exhaust; it should be crisp and have no trace of "woolliness." Black smoke at the exhaust shows that the mixture is much too rich.

2. ADJUSTING PILOT JET. Allow the engine to idle at an excessive speed, with the twist-grip closed and the throttle slide abutting the throttle-stop screw.

Loosen the nut on the throttle-stop adjusting screw, and unscrew the latter until the engine slows up and begins to stall. Then screw the pilot air adjusting screw in or out as required to enable the engine to run regularly and faster.

Next, gently lower the throttle-stop screw until the engine again begins to falter. Now lock the throttle-stop adjusting screw with the lock-nut and commence to readjust the pilot air adjusting screw to obtain the optimum slow-running. Should this second adjustment cause the engine to tick-over at an excessive speed, repeat the adjustment a third time. When perfect slow-running has been obtained, tighten the lock-nut on the throttle-stop screw without disturbing the position of the screw.

3. THE THROTTLE CUT-AWAY. Should appreciable spitting-back at the carburettor occur on accelerating from rest with the engine idling, stop the machine and slightly enrich the mixture by screwing the pilot air adjusting screw in approximately *half a turn*. If this does not effect the desired result, screw it back to its former position and fit a throttle slide having a smaller cut-away.

If there is no spitting-back but the engine jerks under load, this shows an over rich mixture, and the remedy is to fit a throttle slide with larger cut-away, or else to lower the throttle needle.

4. THE NEEDLE POSITION. The tapered needle influences a wide range of throttle openings and affects acceleration. Check performance with the needle in as low a position as possible, i.e. with the clip in the groove nearest the top end of the needle. If acceleration of your Sunbeam declines, and improves by partially closing the strangler, raise the position of the needle by two grooves. If a marked improvement is thereby obtained, try the effect of lowering the needle, by one groove, and leave it in the position where the best performance is obtained.

It should be noted that if the mixture is still excessively rich with the needle clip in groove No. 1 (nearest the top end), wear of the needle jet has probably occurred and renewal of the jet is called for. The needle itself is of stainless steel and wear does not take place, even after a big mileage.

5. FINAL ADJUSTMENT. Also make any final small adjustment which is required to obtain perfectly smooth tick-over, neither too fast nor too slow.

Obstruction in the Pilot Jet. If the pilot jet adjustment does not obtain desired results and the engine will not idle nicely with the throttle almost closed, it is possible that the pilot jet is obstructed. The jet passage, actually a duct drilled in the jet block, is very small and can easily become choked.

To gain access to the pilot jet, remove the jet plug (and two fibre washers) and the float chamber (*see* Fig. 8), and then detach the jet block by pushing it out of the mixing chamber, or tapping it out with a piece of wood. The pilot jet can then be cleared by means of a fine strand of wire.

Bad Slow-running. If it is found impossible to obtain good slow-running by making the pilot air adjustment as described in the second operation on page 25, it is probable that some defect other than carburation is responsible for preventing the engine running slowly at low revolutions. Air leaks are a possible cause which should be looked for (*see* page 22). Badly-seating valves will also weaken the mixture. Defects in the ignition system may also be responsible for poor tick-over. The sparking plugs may be oily, or the points set too close (*see* page 63). Possibly the contact-breaker needs attention (*see* page 64). Examine the distributor and coil connexions, and inspect the h.t. cables for signs of shorting.

Excessive Fuel Consumption. If, in spite of careful checking of the tuning of the carburettor, high fuel consumption continues, it is possible that poor engine compression due to badly fitting piston rings or valves is responsible. Also take into consideration the question of flooding due to a faulty float, air leakage at the joint between the carburettor and manifold and weak valve springs. See that no wastage is caused by slack petrol pipe union nuts.

MAINTENANCE OF THE CARBURETTOR

To ensure correct carburation it is advisable occasionally to remove the carburettor from the engine, strip it down completely, and then thoroughly clean it. It is a good plan to do this about every six months as described below.

To Dismantle the Carburettor. First detach the petrol pipe. Unscrew the jet plug Q (*see* Fig. 7) and remove the float chamber complete. With a box or set spanner, slacken the mixing chamber union nut E. The mixing chamber complete may now be removed from the engine.

To remove the mixing chamber from the manifold, undo the two nuts holding the carburettor flange. Unscrew the mixing chamber lock ring Z (held by clip Z1), and pull out the throttle valve, needle, and air slide (where fitted). Remove the main jet P and the needle jet O. The mixing chamber union nut E may then be removed and the jet block completely pushed out. If this is obstinate, tap gently, using a wooden stump inside the mixing chamber. Unscrew the float chamber cover W, after slackening the lock-screw X. Withdraw the float by pinching the clip V inwards, and pulling the float gently upwards.

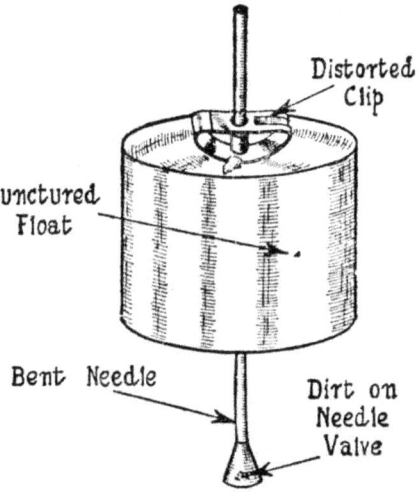

FIG. 10. POSSIBLE CAUSES OF PERSISTENT FLOODING

Cleaning the Carburettor.
Wash all components thoroughly clean with petrol. Pay special attention to the float chamber, and see that any impurities collected inside are removed completely.

Inspecting Components.
If the Amal carburettor has been in continuous service for a considerable period, it is advisable to inspect the following components carefully—

(a) FLOAT CHAMBER. Scrutinize the float chamber components closely. Polish the valve part of the float needle by rotating the needle in its seat while pulling it vertically upwards. If a distinct shoulder is visible on the needle where it seats, renew the needle immediately. Examine the needle for signs of bending.

(b) THROTTLE VALVE. Test in the mixing chamber, and if excessive play is present it is advisable to renew this without delay.

(c) THROTTLE NEEDLE CLIP. This part must securely grip the needle. *Free rotation must not take place*, otherwise the needle groove will become worn and necessitate a new part being fitted. *Be sure to refit the clip in the correct groove.*

(d) JET BLOCK. If trouble has been experienced with erratic

"idling," ascertain by means of a fine strand of wire that the pilot jet *J* (*see* Fig. 7) is clear, and that the pilot outlet *M* in the mixing chamber is unobstructed.

To Assemble the Carburettor. Referring to Fig. 7, refit the jet block *F* with washer on the underside, and screw on lightly the mixing chamber union nut *E*. Screw in the needle jet *O* and the main jet *P*. Open the throttle half-way; grasp the air slide (where fitted) between the thumb and the finger; *make sure that the needle enters the central hole in the barrel H*. Slightly turn the throttle slide until it enters the barrel guide, when on pushing down the slide(s) the air slide should enter its guide. If not, slightly move the mixing chamber cap *Y*, when the air slide will slide into place. Screw on the mixing chamber lock ring *Z*. *No brute force is necessary.*

Attach the carburettor to the cylinder manifold, pushing right home, and examine the washer. Insert the jet plug *Q*, and thoroughly tighten the union nut *E* by means of a fixed spanner. Refit the float and needle, holding the needle head against its seating by means of a pencil until the float and the clip *V* are slipped into position. Make sure that the clip enters the groove provided. Screw on the cover tightly and lock in position by means of the lock-screw *X*. The float-chamber jet plug *Q* has one washer above and one beneath the lug. Screw the jet plug into the union nut *E* and lock securely. Clean the petrol pipe and air filter (if fitted) and replace. It will be necessary to re-check the pilot setting if this has been disturbed.

Needle Jet Wear. The needle itself does *not* become worn. Should the mixture be still too rich with the clip in No. 2 groove (nearest the top end), it is probable that the needle jet requires replacement due to wear. This is assuming that the carburettor has been correctly tuned and that no flooding is taking place.

CHAPTER III

SUNBEAM LUBRICATION

To ensure smooth running and longevity of the engine and machine, it is absolutely imperative to attend to lubrication regularly and conscientiously. The attention normally required is very little, but such attention will prevent any damaging metal-to-metal contact and friction.

ENGINE LUBRICATION

A simple but highly efficient car-type lubrication system of the wet sump type is provided (S7 and S8), and the system is illustrated diagrammatically in Fig. 11. As may be observed, a gear-type oil pump is embodied in the crankshaft rear bearing housing, and is gear-driven direct from the crankshaft. Details of the rear bearing housing and the twin-gear oil pump are clearly shown in Fig. 12. The oil sump itself is of cast aluminium, and has a reinforced gauze filter and a capacity of 3½ pints. It is bolted to the lower face of the crankcase and can readily be detached.

How the Oil Circulates. As regards the circulation of oil inside the Sunbeam engine (a separate supply of oil is used for the gearbox and shaft drive), the oil pump sucks oil from the sump through an extension pipe and a duct machined in the rear bearing housing. The twin-gear pump forces oil upwards to an annular passage encircling the (rear) main bearing, and oil in the annular passage branches off into two separate streams.

One oil stream (*see* Fig. 11) enters via a hole in the (rear) main bearing and an internal annulus, a hole in the periphery of the crankshaft, and thence feeds each pair of big-end crank journals. Surplus oil escapes into the crank chamber, splash-lubricates the cylinder bores, and finally drains to the oil sump after passing the gauze filter.

The second oil stream flows round the annulus encircling the rear main bearing and passes up through vertical ducts to the rear end of the horizontal camshaft. It enters the camshaft through a radially drilled hole in the camshaft rear journal, and proceeds along an axial hole through the middle of the camshaft right to the opposite end to lubricate the camshaft front bearing. The oil now continues along a connecting passage to the hollow rocker shaft. After passing right through the rocker shaft it escapes via radially drilled holes into the overhead rocker bearings. Each bearing has a hole radially drilled so that oil emerges where the rocker and cam make contact.

Surplus oil from the camshaft and overhead rockers collects

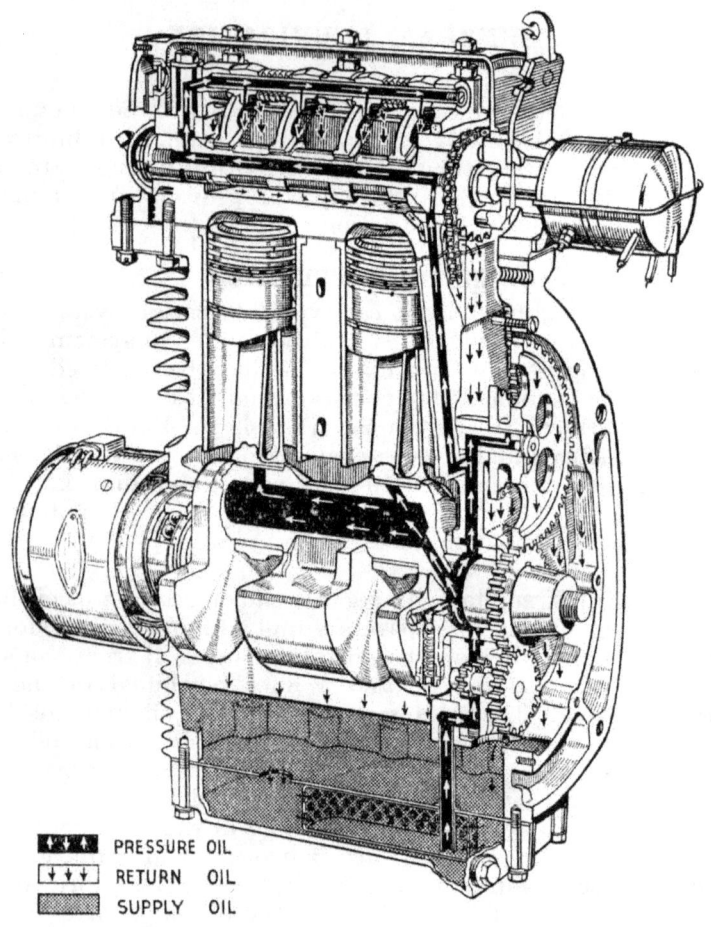

FIG. 11. DIAGRAM SHOWING OIL CIRCULATION IN ENGINE

in a well under the camshaft and returns via ducts down the camshaft driving-chain tunnel. It lubricates the timing gears en route and finally reaches the oil sump after passing the filter.

Inspect the Oil Level in the Sump Weekly. As previously stated, the capacity of the oil sump is 3½ pints. A combined filler cap and dip-stick is conveniently located on the near side

SUNBEAM LUBRICATION

of the crankcase. As may be seen in Fig. 13, the dip-stick has one marking groove only. This indicates the correct oil level.

When your Sunbeam is in regular use, remove the combined filler cap and dip-stick weekly (preferably before setting out on a run) and note whether the oil film adhering to the dip-stick is at or near the correct oil level groove. Always top-up the oil sump with suitable engine oil (*see below*) *before* the level of oil in the sump falls to *half an inch* below the dip-stick groove. Never top-up the oil sump so that the oil level rises above the dip-stick

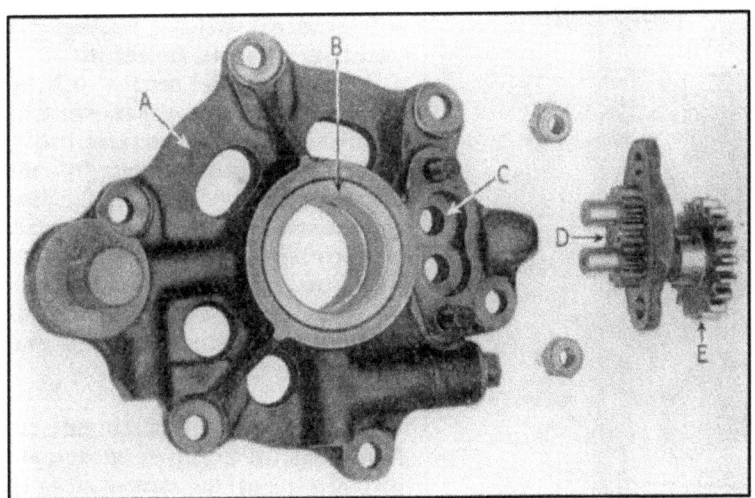

FIG. 12. REAR BEARING HOUSING (WITH BEARING) AND OIL PUMP (REMOVED)
A. Crankshaft rear bearing housing.
B. Crankshaft rear bearing (plain).
C. Oil pump chamber.
D. Oil pump gears.
E. Oil pump driving gear.

mark. Keep a watchful eye on the green warning light (*see page* 8).

Suitable Engine Oils. Always top-up the oil sump with engine oil purchased from branded cabinets or in sealed containers, and make sure that you use the correct grade for summer or winter. To ensure maximum performance and minimum wear, it is best to follow the recommendations of Sunbeam Motor Cycles, Ltd. These are as follows—
 1. Castrol Grand Prix (summer) or XL (winter).
 2. Mobiloil D (summer) or A (winter).
 3. B.P. Energol SAE 50 (summer) or SAE 30 (winter).

4. Shell X-100 50 (summer) or 30 (winter).
5. Esso Extra 40/50 (summer) or 29W/30 (winter).

Note that the above engine oil recommendations are not specified in any order of priority. All five oils are eminently satisfactory for Sunbeams. Having selected a particular brand, it is generally best to continue to use this oil. For use overseas where higher temperatures prevail, different grades (with a higher SAE number) may be desirable.

A motor-cycle engine oil, perhaps not yet as well known as the oils referred to above (and not yet officially recommended by Sunbeam Motor Cycles, Ltd.), is Super Filtrate SAE 50 (summer) or SAE 40 (winter). A Vincent, by the way, using this oil completed an unofficial road test of 20,000 miles without decarbonizing—a most creditable performance.

No Oil Pump Adjustment. The twin-gear oil pump is designed to pressure-feed the correct quantity of oil to the engine at all throttle openings, and therefore has no adjustment. Provided that the pump cover nuts (*see* Fig. 12) are done up tightly and the engine bearings are in reasonably good condition, it is unlikely that any appreciable decline in oil pressure will occur, and the wet sump system will function quite automatically. The normal oil pressure (controlled by a blow-off valve) is 35 lb per sq. in.

It is possible to check the oil circulation (at a point where there is full pressure) by removing the oil-pressure indicator unit and slowly turning the engine over with the kick-starter. This check, however, is rarely necessary and care must be taken, or the engine may become smothered in oil.

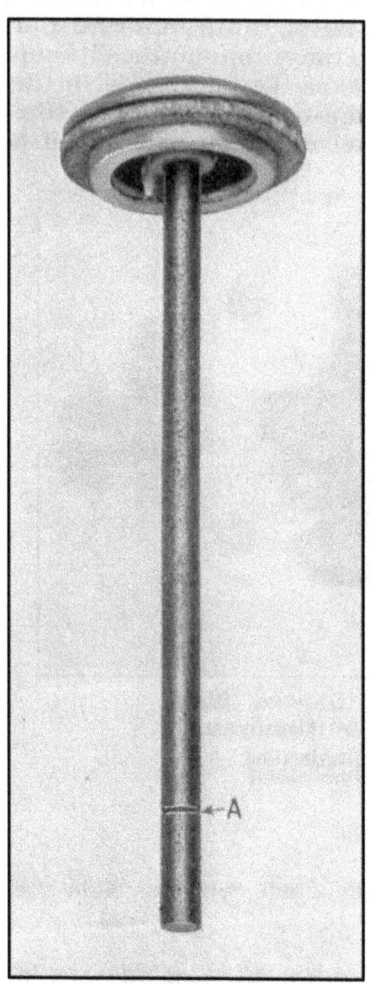

Fig. 13. Sump Filler Cap and Dip-stick

A. Correct level

SUNBEAM LUBRICATION

Drain the Oil Sump Every 2,000 Miles. Do this preferably after a run when the engine oil is still warm. Remove the drain plug located at the rear of the sump on the near side and allow all the old oil to drain away. It is desirable to wash out the sump with suitable flushing oil or thin machine oil. Then after replacing the drain plug replenish the sump with the correct grade of new engine oil to the correct level as indicated by the dip-stick (*see also* page 16).

Clean the Sump Filter at Same Time. It is generally advisable about every 2,000 miles to remove the oil sump and clean the gauze filter thoroughly with petrol or paraffin. Do not use a fluffy rag for cleaning purposes.

To detach the oil sump remove evenly and in a diagonal order the 12 nuts (*see* Fig. 11) which secure it, and then detach the sump together with the filter tray. If you find that the joint washers do not come away with the sump, detach them with great care, and if undamaged, place them aside in a safe place ready for reassembly. If the sump washers should be damaged, however slightly, renew them at once, otherwise oil leakage will almost certainly ensue.

The connecting-rod big-ends are exposed when the filter tray is removed, and it is advisable to cover the under side of the crankcase with a clean cloth pending the replacement of the oil sump and filter tray. See that the 12 nuts retaining the oil sump are securely re-tightened after the sump is replaced.

Oil Pump Driving Gear Removal Not Advised. It is important to note that the oil pump driving gear shown at E in Fig. 12 should not be removed except where this is absolutely essential. The gear is a press fit on its shaft and is secured by a taper pin.

Lubricate the Distributor Unit Every 3,000 Miles. Every 3,000 miles remove the moulded distributor cap and *very lightly* smear the contact-breaker cam (*see* Fig. 34) with grease or engine oil. Also smear a small amount of grease or engine oil on the rocker arm pivot. Avoid excessive lubrication, otherwise some oil or grease may get on the contacts and cause misfiring, and burning of the contacts.

Pull off the moulded rotating arm from the top of the distributor spindle. This exposes a screw which should be removed. Into the screw hole insert a few drops of thin machine oil. Afterwards be careful to fit the screw and the rotating arm correctly. To avoid the risk of burning or tracking it is important to push the rotating arm right home on the distributor spindle.

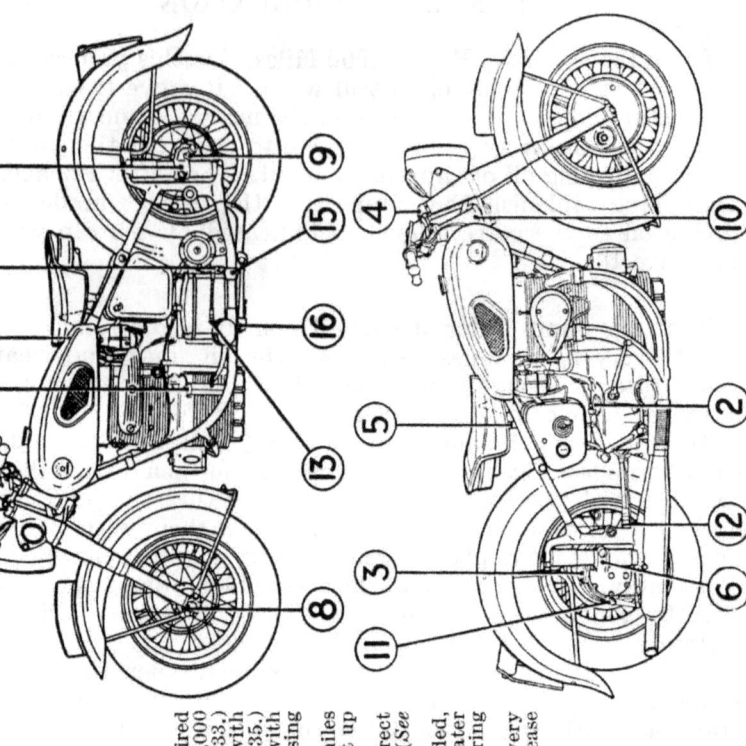

Fig. 14. Lubrication Chart for O.H.C. Sunbeams (1946 onwards)

The only lubrication points not indicated are the distributor unit, controls, and speedometer drive

Key to Lubrication Chart (Fig. 14)

1. *Engine Oil Sump.* Inspect oil level weekly and top-up as required to dip-stick mark. Watch green warning light. Drain sump every 2,000 miles and clean sump filter about every 2,000 miles. (*See* pages 30 and 33.)
2. *Gearbox.* Check oil level weekly and if necessary top-up with engine oil to oil level plug orifice. Drain every 2,000 miles. (*See* page 35.)
3. *Worm Drive.* Verify oil level weekly and top-up as required with suitable oil to oil level plug orifice. If drain plug is fitted, drain casing every 2,000 miles. (*See* page 35.)
4. *Telescopic Front Forks.* If of Sunbeam type, every 1,000 miles remove the top filler plugs, inspect oil level and if necessary top right up with engine oil. Also grease central suspension unit weekly. If of B.S.A. type, drain fork legs and replenish with the correct quantity of suitable oil when excessive fork movement occurs. (*See* pages 37 and 38.)
5. *S7 Saddle Suspension.* Where oil-wick lubrication is provided, annually remove saddle and immerse spring unit in engine oil. On later models with grease lubrication, annually pivot saddle and pack spring unit with grease. (*See* page 39.)
6. *Rear Suspension.* If oil-wick method of lubrication fitted, every 1,000 miles top-up leg reservoirs fully with engine oil. With grease lubrication, apply gun weekly to nipples. (*See* page 38.)
7. *S7 Saddle Pivot.* Grease weekly. (*See* page 40.)
8. *Front Hub.* Grease every 1,000 miles. (*See* page 36.)
9. *Rear Hub.* Grease every 1,000 miles. (*See* page 36.)
10. *Steering Head.* Grease weekly. (*See* page 37.)
11. *Rear Brake Cam Spindle.* Grease weekly. (*See* page 40.)
12. *Rear Universal Joint.* Grease joint weekly. (*See* page 39.)
13. *Rear Brake Pedal.* Grease weekly. (*See* page 40.)
14. *Brake Cross Shaft.* Grease weekly. (*See* page 40.)
15. *Central Stand Pivot.* Grease pivot weekly. (*See* page 40.)
16. *Prop Stand Pivot.* Oil weekly. (*See* page 40.)

SUNBEAM LUBRICATION

No Dynamo Lubrication Necessary. The armature of the Lucas MC45L or MC45 (1946–8 Model S7) dynamo used for ignition and lighting is secured to an extension of the front end of the crankshaft, and pulled up against the front main bearing; automatic lubrication of the bearing is thus provided. No additional lubrication is necessary.

LUBRICATING THE MOTOR-CYCLE PARTS

Though engine lubrication is of primary importance, absence of power losses in the transmission and unfair wear and tear throughout the machine depends upon the correct lubrication of the motorcycle parts, which should never be neglected. A lubrication chart showing all essential lubrication points is given in Fig. 14. This chart should be very carefully studied and acted upon.

Check the Gearbox Oil Level Weekly. Check the oil level and if necessary top-up the gearbox with engine oil (*see* page 31) to the correct level. The gearbox is quite separate from the engine as far as lubrication is concerned, the oil being carried in the lower part of the gearbox and lubricating the gears, dogs, shafts, etc., by splash. The gearbox is designed for *two pints* of engine oil, and an oil level plug enables this quantity of oil to be maintained.

To top-up the gearbox or replenish it after draining (*see below*), remove the filler cap at the top of the box (indicated at 2 in Fig. 14), and also remove the oil level plug at the side of the gearbox. Then pour in engine oil through the filler cap orifice until it starts to run from the level plug orifice. Afterwards replace and tighten *firmly* the filler cap and level plug.

Drain the Gearbox Every 2,000 Miles. About every 2,000 miles remove the drain plug from the base of the gearbox and drain off the whole of the old oil. It is advisable to wash out the gearbox thoroughly with some flushing oil. Then replace the drain plug and fill the gearbox with new engine oil to the height of the level plug orifice. Be careful to tighten the drain plug firmly after replacing it.

The Worm Drive. This, like the gearbox, is self-contained for lubrication purposes. As in the case of the gearbox, weekly remove the filler cap (indicated at 3 in Fig. 14) and if necessary top-up with oil (page 36) till it begins to run from the level plug orifice. Referring to Fig. 15, on Models S8 and S7 de luxe the filler cap D is secured by two screws, and the level plug F is one of seven securing bolts. The worm drive casing, by the way, is designed to hold about *half a pint* of oil. Suitable oils to use for the worm drive are as follows—

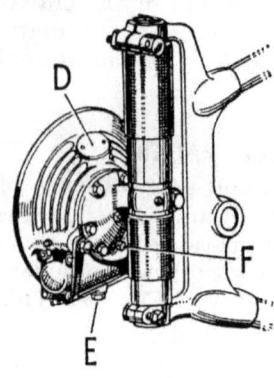

Fig. 15. Worm Drive Lubrication
Drain plug E, omitted on 1946-9 Model S7

Castrol D.
Shell Dentax 140.
Mobilube C.
B.P. Energol SAE 140.
Esso gear oil (heavy).

On Models S8 and S7 de luxe (i.e. from 24th February, 1949, onwards) a drain plug shown at E in Fig. 15 is provided, and this should be removed about every 2,000 miles and the worm drive casing completely drained, washed out with flushing oil and finally replenished with new engine oil to the orifice of the level plug F. Afterwards check that the level plug and drain plug are both *firmly* tightened. Where no drain plug is fitted (i.e. on the original Model S7) it is advisable to drain and wash out the worm drive and casing when a major overhaul is undertaken.

Suitable Greases for the Motor-cycle Parts. Greases recommended by Sunbeam Motor Cycles, Ltd. for the lubrication by means of the grease gun of the various parts are as follows—

Castrolease (heavy).
Mobilgrease No. 2.
Shell Retinax A or C.D.
B.P. Energrease C3.
Esso Grease.

Filling the Grease Gun. The grease gun supplied in the tool kit should be charged so that it is full on the top side of the piston. Grease is obtainable in special canisters having loose collars with a hole in the centre. With this type of grease canister, to charge the grease gun place its barrel over the hole in the central floating plate and press firmly downwards. Turn the grease gun and simultaneously remove it from the floating plate. This procedure will charge the grease gun flush with the top of the barrel. Afterwards replace the screwed cap. Where no special canister is available, charge the barrel of the grease gun by hand, using a suitable lath or implement.

Grease the Hubs Every 1,000 Miles. The front and rear wheel hubs have ball journal bearings and these require to be greased

SUNBEAM LUBRICATION

about every 1,000 miles. Oil must not be used. With the grease gun inject suitable grease (*see* opposite) through the grease nipple provided in the centre of each hub. Three to four strokes of the grease gun should be quite sufficient. If you over-lubricate, there is a risk of grease getting on to the brake linings and causing brake inefficiency.

Steering Head Lubrication. Apply the grease gun weekly to the nipple (indicated at 10 in Fig. 14). Two to three strokes should suffice. The top bearing is packed with grease on assembly, and

Fig. 16. Lubrication of Telescopic Forks
(1946–9 Sunbeam type)

as this bearing does not take the load, further lubrication is not normally called for, and a grease nipple is therefore omitted.

Front Forks (1946–9 Sunbeam Type). On the original Model S7 apply the grease gun weekly to the nipple on the top bolt of the central suspension spring unit and give a few strokes. The nipple is shown at *A* in Fig. 16, also at *D* in Fig. 47. Also about every 1,000 miles remove the top filler plug and inspect and top up the oil in each front fork leg *B*.

Wick lubrication is provided for the telescopic front fork legs. The central column of each fork leg is packed with cotton wick soaked in oil. A reservoir immediately above each column of wick maintains a supply of lubricant for the wick for a very long period, and effectively lubricates the bearings of the telescopic tubes. Thus to ensure correct fork lubrication, it is only necessary to keep each wick impregnated with oil. To replenish each fork leg, remove the filler plug and top right up with engine oil. Afterwards replace the filler plug and tighten it firmly.

Front Forks (1949–57 B.S.A. Type). The telescopic front forks on Models S8 and S7 de luxe are of quite different design to the Sunbeam type provided on the original Model S7. If after a considerable mileage excessive up and down movement develops, it is advisable to drain each fork leg and replenish it to the correct level, using the under-mentioned procedure.

Remove the large hexagon-headed cap (shown at 4 in Fig. 14) from the top of each fork leg. Also unscrew and remove the small drain plug indicated by an arrow in Fig. 17. It is convenient to drain both fork legs together. To assist complete draining, stand astride the Sunbeam, grasp the handlebars, and work the forks up and down. After all trace of oil has been drained from both fork legs, screw home the two small drain plugs, refill each fork leg to the correct level, and replace the hexagon-headed caps on the top of the fork legs.

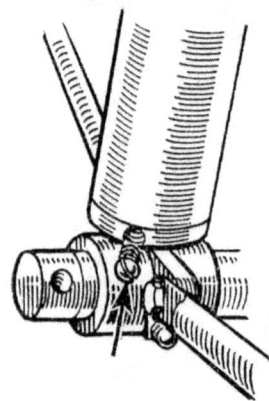

Fig. 17. Drain Plug on Telescopic Forks (1949–57 B.S.A. type)

On 1949–55 Model S8 the correct amount of oil to insert is *one quarter* of a pint, but on the 1949–55 Model S7 de luxe the correct quantity is *one-third* of a pint. Note that the insertion of slightly more than the amounts just quoted is not detrimental, but on no account must you fill the fork legs completely. On 1956–7 Models S7 and S8 insert 7½ fluid ounces. Sunbeam Motor Cycles, Ltd. recommend the use of one of the following oils—

Castrolite.
Shell X-100 20.
Mobiloil Arctic.
B.P. Energol SAE 20.
Esso Extra 20W/30.

Rear Suspension (1946–7 Model S7). Up to June, 1947, an oil-wick method of lubrication, identical to that used on the original Sunbeam type front forks, was used; about every 1,000 miles remove the filler plugs from the top of the suspension unit upper members and top-up each telescopic leg reservoir *fully* with engine oil (*see* page 31).

Rear Suspension (1947–57 Models S7, S8, and S7 de luxe). Subsequent to 21st July, 1947, all Sunbeams have grease gun lubrication provided for the rear suspension, and it is advisable to apply the grease gun weekly to the grease nipples indicated at 6 in Fig. 14. Give a few strokes. Little and often is the best method of lubricating the rear suspension.

Grease the Rear Universal Joint Weekly. Apply the grease gun weekly to the rear universal joint nipple indicated at 12 in Fig. 14, and at *B* in Fig. 51. Two to three strokes of the gun should be sufficient.

Saddle Suspension (1946–9 Model S7). Up to March, 1949, a wick method of lubricating the saddle suspension was employed. Replenishment of the oil is advised annually, the supply being

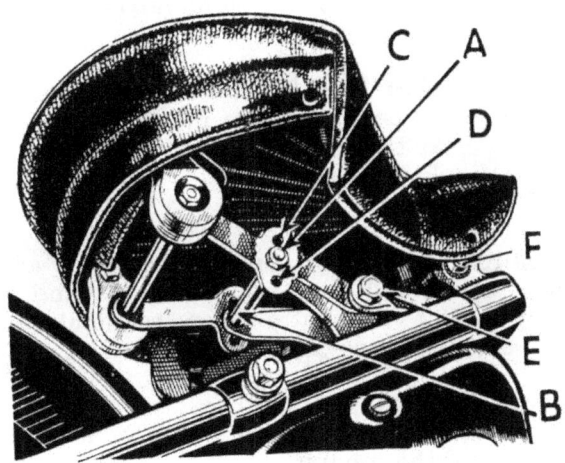

FIG. 18. SADDLE SUSPENSION (1946–9 MODEL S7)
Not applicable to Model S8. The 1949–57 Model S7 de luxe saddle suspension is shown in Fig. 38

enough to last for a whole season's riding. Replenishment involves removing the saddle and withdrawing the spring unit, because the latter is almost horizontal and is enclosed in the top frame tube. The removal procedure is as below.

Referring to Fig. 18, remove the top bolts *E* and *F* and detach the saddle. Also withdraw the spring unit from its housing in the top tube of the frame. Immerse the unit in engine oil for approximately 12 hours, replace the unit in its housing, and finally fit the saddle.

Saddle Suspension (1949–57 Model S7 de luxe). Subsequent to 9th September, 1949, the oil-wick method of lubricating the S7 saddle suspension was modified in favour of grease lubrication. As with the oil-wick system, replenishment of the grease is not possible with the saddle *in situ*, because of the horizontal position and enclosure of the spring unit.

It is advisable to replenish the grease annually. To do this, remove the single bolt E (Fig. 18) and pivot the saddle upwards on its nose bolt until you can draw out to the maximum[1] the spring unit from the top frame tube. Now pack the unit with grease (which should last for a full season), replace it in its housing, and finally refit the saddle.

Do not forget to apply the grease gun about once a week to the nipple (1950-1) or two nipples (1952 onwards) provided for the external moving parts of the saddle linkage. Pay special attention to the nipple in the centre of the saddle pivot indicated at 7 in Fig. 14.

Lubricate the Brakes Weekly. Referring to Fig. 14, inject weekly two or three shots of grease into the nipple 13 for the rear brake pedal. At the same time inject a similar amount of grease into the nipple for the brake cross shaft 14 and the nipple for the rear brake cam spindle 11.

Oil the Controls, Rod Joints, and Cables. It is advisable, to ensure smooth action and to prevent rusting, to apply an oil-can (containing cycle oil) to the control levers, rod joints, and exposed cables. Use only a few drops of oil at each point.

The Speedometer Drive. At monthly intervals (say every 1,000 miles) it is advisable to unscrew the top of the flexible drive and pour engine oil into the conduit.

Leakage at Oil Indicator Unit. Should persistent leakage of oil occur at the oil indicator unit (shown just below the cam-chamber baffle in Fig. 53), this can be cured by fitting a modified indicator unit (Part No. 89-496).

Do Not Forget the Stands. Referring to Fig. 14, weekly grease the central stand pivot 15, and oil the prop stand pivot 16.

[1] Note that if, for some reason other than lubrication, you wish to remove the spring unit completely, you must first remove the rear mudguard from the machine.

CHAPTER IV

CARE OF THE LIGHTING SYSTEM

THIS chapter covers the components of the lighting system only, those items concerned with the coil ignition system (except the battery which is responsible for both lighting and ignition) being dealt with in Chapter V. All 1946 and later Sunbeam Twins have similar Lucas electrical equipment.

The Lucas Equipment (1946 Onwards). Models, S7, S8, and S7 de luxe all have a modern type high output MC45 (MC45L, 1949 onwards) Lucas dynamo with its armature mounted on an extension of the crankshaft (located by a dowel and secured by a bolt with l.h. thread). The yoke, pole shoe, and field coil assembly is spigoted into the crankcase and secured by countersunk-headed screws.

The dynamo is of the compensated voltage control type, the MCR1 (MCR2, 1949 onwards) C.V.C. unit with cut-out (and ignition coil) being mounted on the control panel adjacent to the toolbox below the saddle. The unit ensures that the dynamo output varies according to the load on the battery and its state of charge. The battery is a Lucas lead-acid type PUW7E with its positive connexion earthed to the frame of the Sunbeam.

The "business end" of the lighting system includes a Lucas type MS142 headlamp mounted on the telescopic front fork brackets. Its lighting switch and the ammeter are mounted on the control panel below the saddle. The tail lamp or stop-tail lamp is also of Lucas design, and the same applies to the weatherproof electric horn which announces one's approach in no uncertain manner. Useful pictorial wiring diagrams of the complete electrical equipment are shown in Figs. 25 and 26.

DYNAMO MAINTENANCE

Before interfering with the wiring, it is advisable to disconnect the connector close to the *negative* terminal of the battery. Pull back the rubber shield and unscrew the cable connector. When doing this be sure that it does not touch any metal part of the Sunbeam frame, or the battery will be effectively short-circuited.

Inspect the Commutator Brushes Every 12,000 Miles. The carbon brushes must always make good electrical contact with the copper segments of the commutator. About every 12,000 miles remove the two screws (three, 1949–57) securing the dynamo end cover, take off the cover, and check that the two carbon

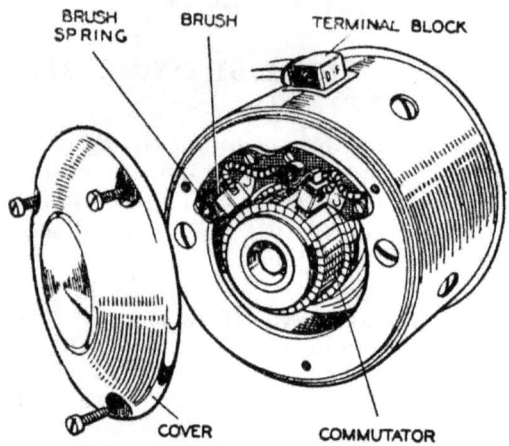

Fig. 19. Commutator Brushgear
(MC45 dynamo on 1946–8 Model S7)

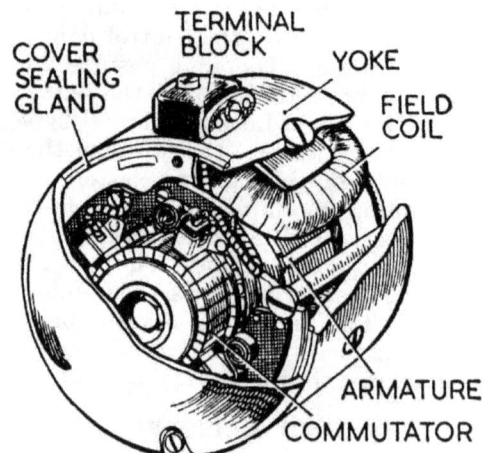

Fig. 20. Commutator Brushgear
(MC45L dynamo on 1949–57 Models S7, S7 de luxe, and S8)

brushes (four on MC45L dynamo) move quite freely in their box-type holders. To do this, hold back the brush-retaining springs and gently pull and release the flexible connecting leads (*see* Figs. 19 and 20). If a brush tends to stick, remove it from its holder

CARE OF THE LIGHTING SYSTEM

and clean its sides thoroughly with a cloth moistened with petrol. When removing a brush by holding back its retaining spring and pulling on its lead, see that the brush-retaining spring is in fact quite clear of the brush holder.

Inspect the contact faces of the brushes and clean them thoroughly. The faces should be uniformly polished. Examine the brushes for wear and unevenness. Renew brushes which have worn so much that they no longer bed down properly on the commutator. New brushes should be bedded down at a Lucas service depot. Brushes which do not require renewal must always be replaced in their original positions so as to preserve their "bedding."

It is good practice to renew carbon brushes *before* serious wear becomes apparent, as this will prevent sparking and blackening of the commutator segments. Check that the two brush-retaining springs have not lost their tension and exert adequate pressure on the brushes. Never fit brushes or springs other than those of the correct type recommended for the particular dynamo.

The Commutator. It is important to keep the surface of the commutator clean and free from oil, brush dust, and dirt. If oil or grease should get on the segments, this would cause sparking and accelerate the collection of impurities in the grooves between the segments. About every 12,000 miles remove one of the commutator brushes and examine the segments, which should be highly polished and dark bronze in colour.

If the commutator segments are dirty, clean them by removing a brush from its holder and pressing a fine dry duster against the commutator (through the holder) with a suitable piece of wood while slowly rotating the engine. If the commutator is very dirty, moisten the duster with petrol.

When replacing the dynamo end cover, carefully position the rubber cover sealing gland between the cover and yoke (*see* Fig. 20), and tighten the fixing screws evenly.

Compensated Voltage Control. The C.V.C. unit mounted in the control panel adjacent to the toolbox automatically gives a high dynamo output when the battery is in a discharged condition. A quick recharge soon restores the battery to normal. There is no possible chance of over-charging occurring. When the lamps are switched on, a compensating increase in charging occurs. When the battery is well charged the C.V.C. unit gives only a trickle charge sufficient to meet current demands and keep the battery in good shape. In all three switch positions (*see* page 46) a controlled dynamo output occurs.

At low engine r.p.m. current is prevented from flowing back

to the battery by the cut-out, which opens. When the r.p.m. increase sufficiently to permit the dynamo to charge the battery, the cut-out closes and the circuit is completed. Do not meddle with the C.V.C. unit. No adjustment is normally required after the unit is correctly set and sealed by the makers.

Ammeter Readings. On all O.H.C. Sunbeams a centre-zero ammeter is mounted on the front of the control panel (together with the lighting switch and ignition switch). It provides an indication of the current flowing out of or into the battery, and its readings give a check on the functioning of the charging equipment.

Note that because of the inclusion of the C.V.C. unit, the ammeter charge readings are seldom high. During normal daytime running the dynamo gives only a trickle charge and the ammeter needle seldom indicates more than one or two amperes.

CARE OF THE BATTERY

The lamps, horn, and coil ignition system depend upon the battery being cared for. Its neglect soon causes trouble and depreciation of the cells. But in practice very little attention is needed to keep the battery thoroughly serviceable.

Top-up the Cells Regularly. Examine the acid level about every four weeks, and even more frequently in tropical climates. Release the battery clamp, take off the battery lid, and remove the filler plugs. Inspect the vent hole in each plug and make certain that it is not obstructed. A choked vent hole will result in an increase of pressure in the cell owing to "gassing," and this may cause trouble.

Wipe the top of the battery clean with a rag and also verify that the rubber washer fitted beneath each filler plug, to prevent leakage, is in position. After wiping the top of the battery, either destroy the rag or wash it thoroughly, using several changes of water. See that a supply of clean distilled water is to hand.

Be careful not to hold a naked light near the vents. If the level is below the tops of the separators, add *distilled* water[1] with a Lucas battery filler or a hydrometer as required to bring the level correct (*see* Fig. 21). This should be done just before a charge run, as the agitation due to running and the gassing will thoroughly mix the solution. Avoid spilling any water on the top of the battery. Acid must not be added to the electrolyte unless the solution has been spilled. If the solution has been spilled by

---

[1] The distilled water, unlike the acid, is lost gradually by evaporation. Bottles of distilled water can be obtained from most garages and from chemists.

CARE OF THE LIGHTING SYSTEM

accident, it is advisable to have the battery examined at a Lucas service depot.

Check the Specific Gravity Occasionally. Occasionally hydrometer readings (specific gravity values) should be taken of the solution in each of the cells. The method of doing this is shown in

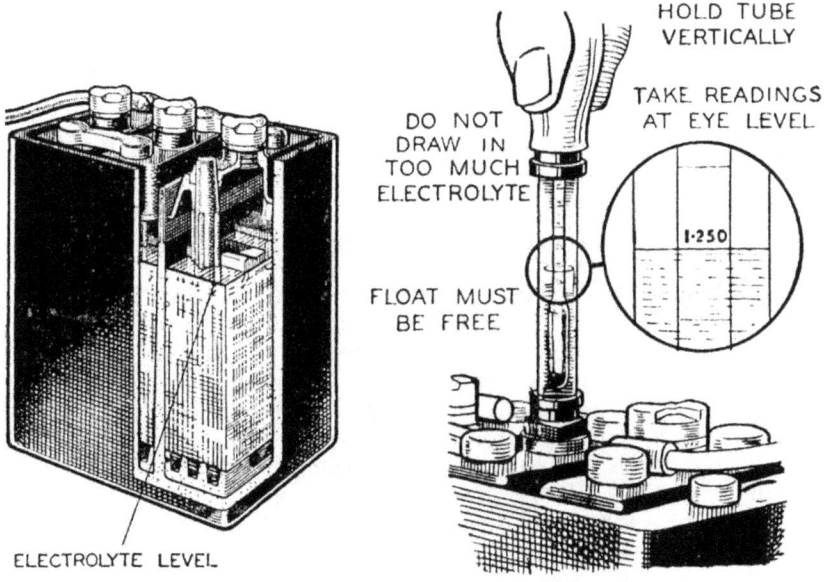

Fig. 21. Keep Electrolyte Level with Tops of Battery Separators

Fig. 22. Checking Specific Gravity of Electrolyte with Lucas Hydrometer

(*Joseph Lucas, Ltd.*)

Fig. 22. The Lucas hydrometer contains a graduated float which indicates the specific gravity of the battery cell from which a sample of electrolyte is taken.

After a sample has been taken and checked, it must, of course, be returned to the cell. The taking of S.G. readings with a hydrometer is the most efficient way of ascertaining the state of charge of the battery. The S.G. readings should be approximately the *same for all three cells*. Should the reading for one cell differ substantially from the readings for the others, probably some acid has been spilled or has leaked from the cell concerned. There is also a possibility of a short-circuit between the battery plates. In the latter case it will be necessary to return the battery to a Lucas depot for attention.

Under no circumstances must the battery be permitted to

remain in a discharged condition for long, or serious deterioration will occur. After checking the S.G. readings and topping-up the cells, wipe the top of the battery and remove any spilled electrolyte or water; replace the three filler plugs and the battery lid. Then fit and tighten the battery clamping screw.

The Battery Connexions. Always keep the battery connexions clean, free from corrosion, and tight, otherwise the ammeter readings will *not* indicate the true state of charge of the battery. To prevent corrosion they should be smeared with petroleum jelly.

Correct Readings. With Lucas batteries fitted to Sunbeam machines, the specific gravity readings at an acid temperature of approximately 60°F should be: 1·280–1·300, battery fully charged; about 1·210, battery about half discharged; below 1·150, battery fully discharged.

Never leave the battery in a discharged state for any appreciable period. A low state of charge is often caused through parking the machine for long periods with the lighting switch in the "L" position, unaccompanied by much daylight running. The remedy is, of course, to undertake more daylight running and to keep the switch in the "Off" position as much as possible until the battery is restored to its normal state of charge. If overcharging should occur, have the C.V.C. unit examined. If you put your Sunbeam out of service for an appreciable period, first see that the battery is fully charged and then give it a refreshing charge about once a fortnight (if necessary from an independent source of electrical supply).

THE LAMPS, BULBS, ETC.

As the safety of the rider at night depends on his lamps, it is most important to keep them in good condition.

The Lucas MS142 Headlamp. This headlamp is provided on all 1946 and subsequent Sunbeams and has a built-in speedometer and green and red warning lights (*see* page 8) concerned with the lubrication and ignition systems respectively. The headlamp is of the focusing type and has the usual main and pilot bulb arrangement. The pilot bulb is, of course, intended for riding in well lit streets and for parking purposes, while the main bulb provides a powerful beam for all other purposes. To prevent dazzle, the main bulb has two filaments, with the dipped beam filament controlled by a switch on the handlebars (*see* Figs. 4 and 5).

The Lighting Switch. The lighting switch is mounted (with the ignition switch and ammeter) on the front of the control panel

CARE OF THE LIGHTING SYSTEM

adjacent to the toolbox and has the following switch positions—
"Off"—All lamps switched off.
"Low"—Headlamp pilot bulb, tail lamp, and sidecar lamp (where fitted) on.
"High"—Headlamp main bulb, tail lamp, and sidecar lamp (where fitted) on.

Note that, with the lighting switch turned to any of the above positions, the dynamo continues to charge the battery, the C.V.C. unit controlling the amount of charging as required.

Alignment of the Headlamp. It is important to see that the headlamp is kept correctly aligned. To verify the alignment, take your Sunbeam to a level stretch of road, turn the lighting switch to the "High" position, and the dip switch to the "Up" position. If the alignment is correct, the projected beam should be parallel with the road, or very slightly depressed. If incorrect, loosen the two headlamp-securing bolts and move the lamp in its fork brackets as required. When alignment is correct, firmly retighten the two bolts.

Focusing the Headlamp. On new Sunbeams the double-filament main bulb is correctly focused at the works and, provided that genuine Lucas replacement bulbs of the correct type are used, it should

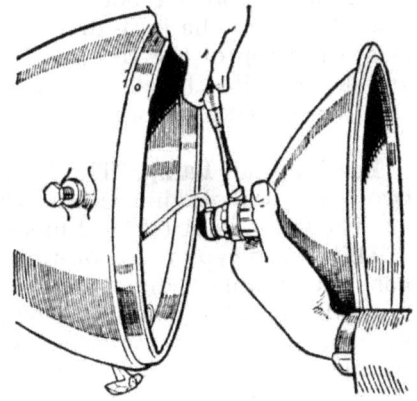

FIG. 23. FOCUSING ADJUSTMENT ON LUCAS HEADLAMPS

not be necessary to alter the original focusing adjustment. Where a correct Lucas replacement bulb is not available, or if for any reason the focusing adjustment has been disturbed, it is desirable to refocus the headlamp in the following manner—

Remove the lamp front and reflector (page 48). Then with a screwdriver loosen the clamping screw (*see* Fig. 23) on the clip at the back of the reflector and push the bulb holder in or out as required. It may be necessary to make several focusing adjustments. After effecting each adjustment, replace the lamp front and reflector. Test the beam for focus. When you obtain the correct focus, retighten firmly the screw on the bulb-holder clamping clip.

Correct Focus. The headlamp on your Sunbeam is correctly focused when the reflected rays of light are about parallel and when the beam thrown on a light-coloured wall about 40 ft away illuminates brightly a circular area of minimum diameter. To obtain a parallel beam, the filament for the main driving beam should be as near as possible to the focal point of the reflector. Should the filament be positioned in front of the focal point, a converging beam (with dark centre) results. If the filament is positioned behind the focal point, a diverging beam occurs. Both diverging and converging beams give poor road illumination and are likely to dazzle other road users. If the headlamp beam lacks uniformity, has a short range, and a dark centre, refocus the headlamp immediately.

To Remove the Headlamp Front and Reflector. To detach the front and reflector from the Lucas MS142 headlamp, pull forward the fixing clip at the bottom of the headlamp and withdraw the assembly from the bottom of the lamp first. When replacing it, locate the top of the rim first, and then press on at the bottom and secure with the clip. To remove the bulb holder, press back the two securing springs.

The Stop-tail Lamp. The Lucas type 477-1 stop-tail lamp has two bulbs. To obtain access to the bulbs, turn to the left and pull out the lamp front (1951–2 models).

The Lucas type 525 stop-tail lamp fitted to 1953–5 Sunbeams has one double-filament bulb. The 3-watt filament gives the normal rear light and number plate illumination, while the 18-watt filament, used in conjunction with a specially designed thermoplastic cover, gives an intense red illumination for the braking warning signal. To obtain access to the double-filament bulb, remove the two screws securing the plastic cover; you can then withdraw the bulb from its bayonet fixing.

The Warning Lights. To obtain access to the bulbs of the red and green warning lights for the coil ignition and lubrication systems, it is only necessary to unscrew the covers carrying the coloured glasses.

Bulb Renewal. Be careful to fit none but Lucas bulbs designed for correct focusing with Lucas reflectors. Make sure that the replacement is of the correct type. It is generally wise to renew the headlamp bulb after long service *before* it actually burns out, because if sagging of the filaments occurs it will never be in proper focus.

The metal caps of Lucas bulbs are marked with a number for identification purposes and it is important when renewing a bulb to verify that it has the correct number marked on its cap (e.g.

CARE OF THE LIGHTING SYSTEM

No. 70). When renewing a double-filament main bulb it is essential to see that it is fitted the correct way round, i.e. with the dipped beam filament *above* the centre filament. On Lucas main bulbs the word "Top" is etched so as to indicate the correct position for the bulb in its holder. The correct bulb renewals are as follows—

HEADLAMP MAIN BULB—On the 1946-9 Model S7 (with Sunbeam type front forks) fit a 6 volt, 24/24 watt, Lucas No. 70 double-filament S.B.C. main bulb. In the case of 1949 and subsequent Models S8 and S7 de luxe (with B.S.A. type front forks), the correct main bulb replacement for the headlamp is a 6 volt, 30/30 watt, Lucas No. 169 double-filament S.B.C. bulb.

HEADLAMP PILOT BULB—On all Sunbeam models fit a 6 volt, 3 watt Lucas No. 200 bulb.

WARNING LIGHTS—If the two warning lights in the headlamp of all Sunbeam models require renewal, use a 2·5 volt, 0·2 amp Lucas No. C252A screw-cap type.

TAIL LAMP. Fit a 6 volt, 3 watt, Lucas No. 200 bayonet-fixing bulb. Always carry a spare bulb.

STOP-TAIL LAMP—Fit a 6 volt, 6/18 watt, No. 384 bayonet-type bulb.

SIDECAR LAMP (WHERE FITTED)—Fit the same type of Lucas bulb as required for the headlamp pilot (*see above*).

THE ELECTRIC HORN

The Lucas HF1234 electric horn fitted to all Sunbeams is very carefully adjusted at the works and will give a long period of satisfactory service without further attention. After a very long time, however, some wear of the vibrating parts may occur, causing roughness and loss of tone. This can be rectified by a simple adjustment.

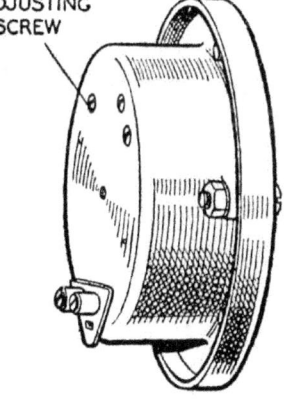

FIG. 24. TONE ADJUSTMENT ON LUCAS HORN (1946-57)

External Sources of Trouble. Should the horn become silent or emit a choking sound, do not assume at once that the instrument itself is at fault. Some external cause may be to blame. Possible causes of such trouble are: a loose connexion or short-circuit in the wiring of the horn, a run-down battery, or a faulty horn button caused possibly through corrosion. There is also the possibility of poor horn functioning being caused through the horn fixing bolt becoming slack. This point can be checked by

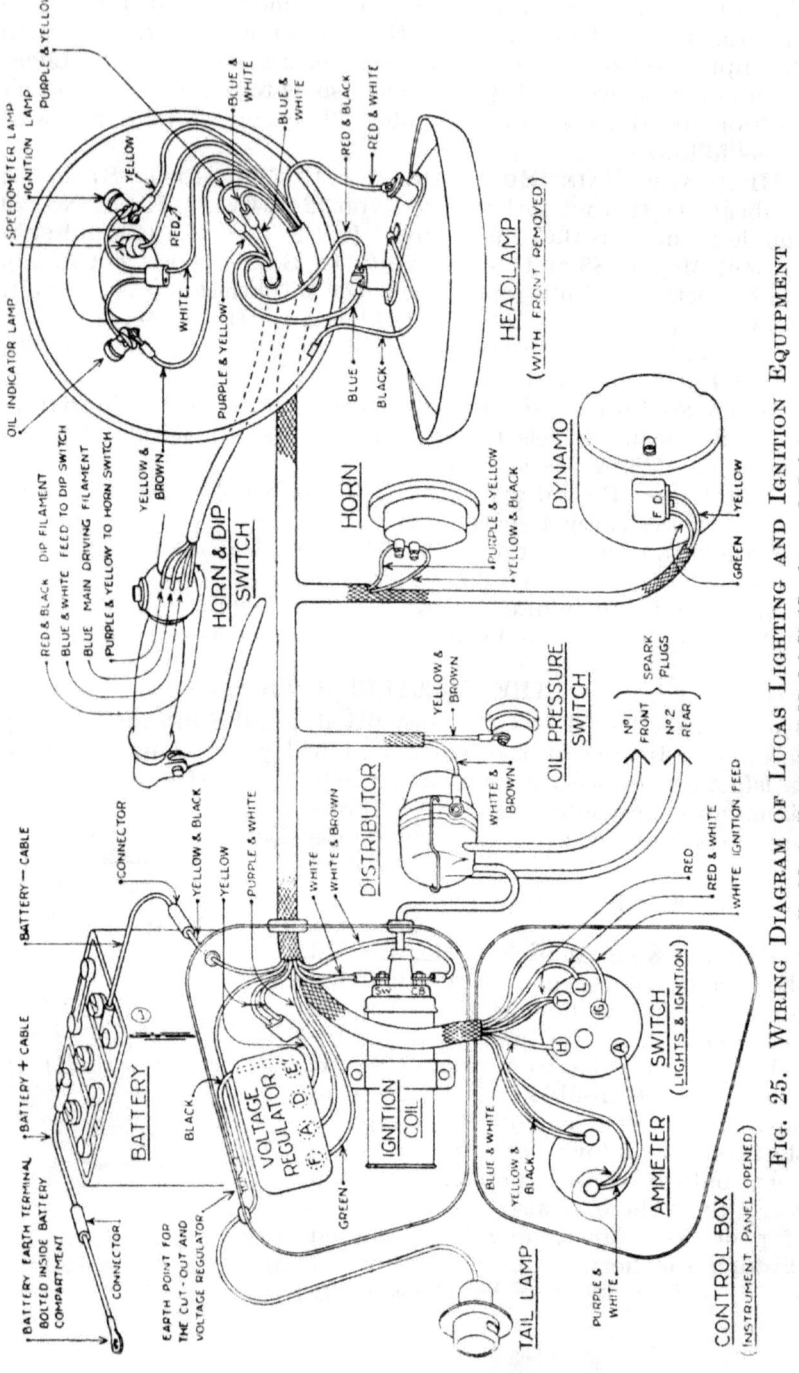

Fig. 25. Wiring Diagram of Lucas Lighting and Ignition Equipment
Applicable to the 1946-9 Model S7 (Sunbeam forks)

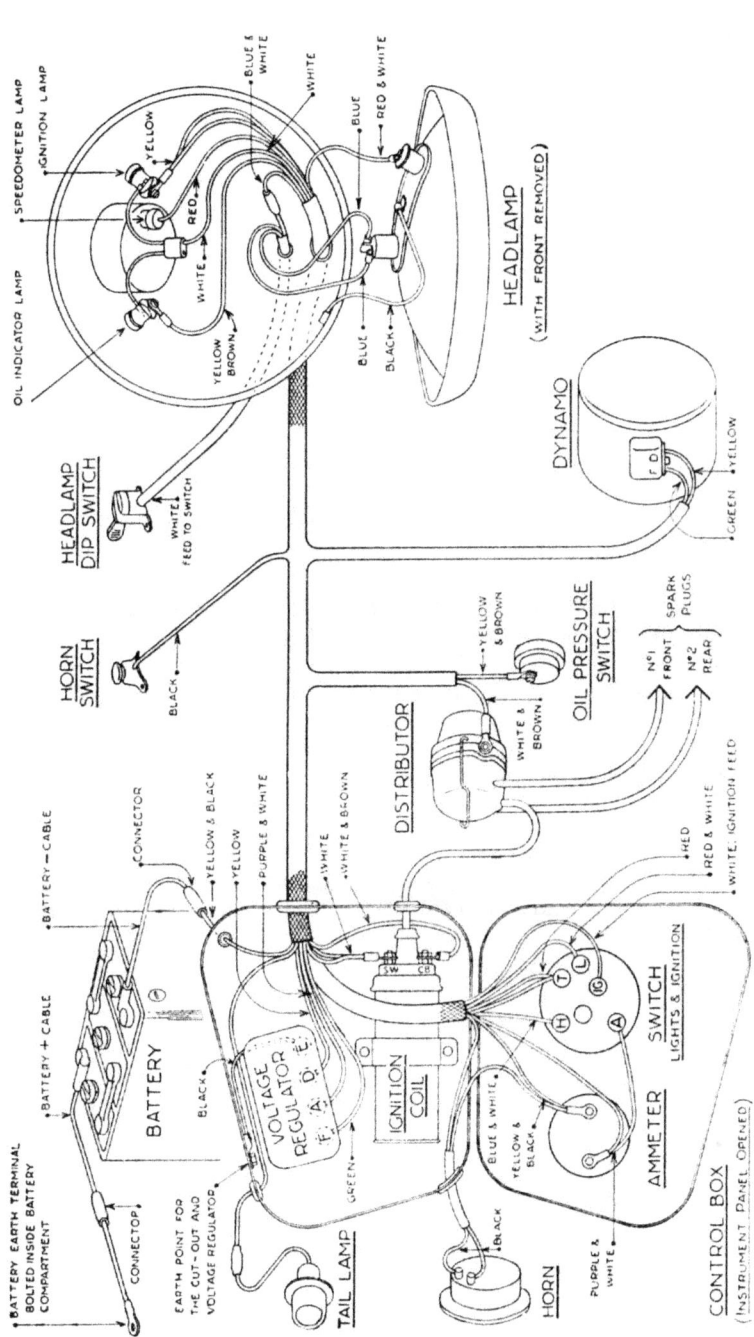

FIG. 26. WIRING DIAGRAM OF LUCAS LIGHTING AND IGNITION EQUIPMENT
Applicable to the 1949 and subsequent Models S8 and S7 de luxe

removing the horn, gripping its body firmly in the hand, and pressing the horn button switch.

Adjusting the Lucas Horn. Though a tone adjustment is rarely called for, an adjustment can be made in the following manner. With a small screwdriver turn the adjusting screw[1] shown in Fig. 24 *two or three notches.* It is generally necessary to turn the screw *clockwise* and, to facilitate the adjustment, the under side of the screw is serrated. Check the horn's tone and make a further adjustment if necessary. Be careful not to make an excessive adjustment, otherwise the contacts may not separate. Make no attempt to tamper with the nut securing the tone disk or with any screws other than the one referred to above.

After an Adjustment. Operate the horn and note its current consumption. This should not exceed 4–5 amp. If no sound is audible, do not continue to depress the horn button. Perhaps the contacts are failing to close through an excessive adjustment, and the remedy is to make a further adjustment.

Compulsory Red Reflectors. Sunbeam owners should note that the law requires that *all* solo motor-cycles shall carry at the rear a red reflector (of 1½ in. minimum diameter) in addition to (or combined with) the tail lamp or stop-tail lamp. Where a sidecar is fitted, this must carry an *additional* red reflector at the rear.

Extra Tail Lamp on Sidecar Outfits. In the case of all sidecars, a tail lamp as well as a red reflector must now be fitted *in addition* to those provided on the motor-cycle itself.

[1] The horn on some earlier Sunbeams has two instead of three screws on its back. In this case the adjuster screw is the extreme left-hand one also.

CHAPTER V

GENERAL MAINTENANCE AND OVERHAUL

THE general maintenance and overhauling instructions in this chapter apply to all 1946 and subsequent models, except where the instructions are specifically dated. As regards carburation, lubrication, and the lighting system, detailed maintenance instructions have already been given in preceding chapters, and this chapter therefore contains only cross-references to these subjects. Full instructions are given on routine adjustments, decarbonizing, major overhaul, etc.

Spares and Repairs. Should you have occasion to forward or deliver parts (either for repair or as patterns) to Sunbeam Motor Cycles, Ltd. (service, spares, and repair department) or to a Sunbeam spares and repairs specialist, do not forget to attach to each part a label clearly bearing your full name and address. With your accompanying instructions do not omit to quote the *complete* engine or frame number, according to the part concerned (*see* page 2). In correspondence with Sunbeam Motor Cycles, Ltd. concerning your machine, you should also include the name and address of the dealer from whom you bought your S7 or S8, the date of purchase, and the index letters and registration numbers.

Sunbeam Spares Stockists in London Area. The following appointed stockists maintain a comprehensive range of Sunbeam spares: Whitbys of Acton, Ltd.; Lovetts, Ltd.; Naylor & Root, Ltd.; Kays of Ealing, Ltd.; Harry Nash Motors, Ltd.; E. Beckett; Glanfield Lawrence, Ltd.; W. E. Humphreys, Ltd.; Millars Motors (Mitcham), Ltd.; and Slocomb's, Ltd.

Items Required for Maintenance. For the proper maintenance of your motor-cycle there are a number of items which you must have handy in the garage or lock-up. These include: a tin or carton of suitable engine oil (*see* page 31) for engine and gearbox lubrication, a tin or carton of gear oil (*see* page 36) for worm drive lubrication, a canister of suitable grease (*see* page 36) for the grease-gun lubrication of the cycle parts, a small oil-can containing cycle oil for control lubrication, a convenient tin or drip-tray for draining the engine sump and gearbox, a can of paraffin for general cleaning, some miscellaneous dishes or jars for washing small components in, a stiff brush for scouring dirt off the sump, some non-fluffy rags, two chamois leathers for

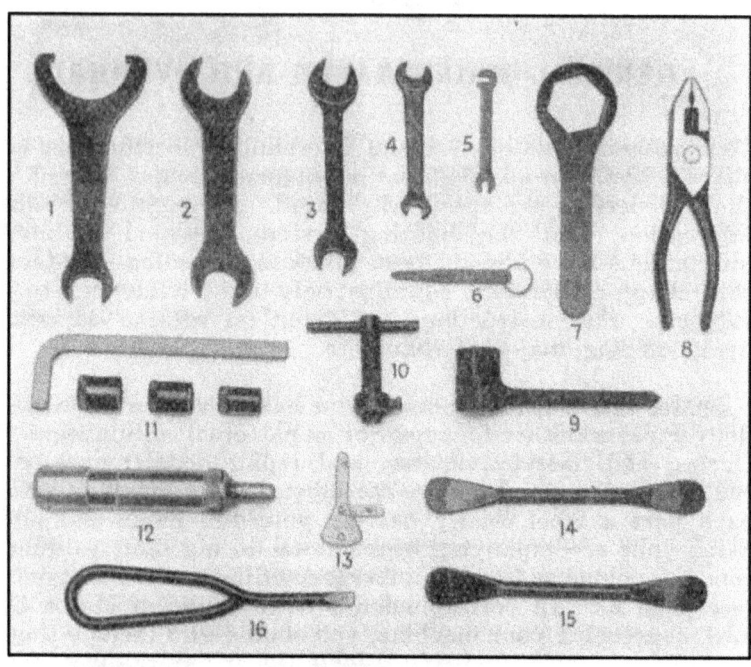

Fig. 27. The Model S8 Tool Kit (1949 onwards)

From September, 1950, a plain tommy bar (not shown) is included. The Models S7 and S7 de luxe Sunbeam tool kits are similar to the Model S8 kit shown, but include different tyre levers. Kits for 1946-9 S7 models (with Sunbeam-type front forks) have the two spanners shown at 2 and 3 in Fig. 28. All S7 and S8 tool kits up to June, 1950, also contain the two spanners shown at 1 and 4 in Fig. 28

Key to Fig. 27

1. Spanner for exhaust pipe unions and body of oil switch.
2. Double-ended spanner.
3. Double-ended spanner.
4. Double-ended spanner.
5. Spanner for valve clearances.
6. Feeler gauge (0·018 in.) for valve clearances.
7. Spanner for top nuts on telescopic fork legs.
8. Pliers (wire-cutting type).
9. Sparking plug spanner and screwdriver.
10. Tool for grinding-in valves (suction-type tool supplied in 1953 kit).
11. Wrench with three socket spanners.
12. Grease gun.
13. Lucas screwdriver with feeler gauge (0·012 in.) for contact-breaker.
14. Tyre lever.
15. Tyre lever.
16. Metal screwdriver.

cleaning the enamel and chromium, a sponge and pail, some soft dusters (preferably of the selvyt type), a tin of good wax polish for brightening up the enamelled parts, and a tin of good hand cleanser in case paraffin proves insufficient to remove all dirt.

GENERAL MAINTENANCE AND OVERHAUL 55

You should also have available a suitable tyre pressure gauge (*see* page 68), a good tyre repair outfit, some distilled water and a battery filler for topping-up the battery, a hydrometer for testing the specific gravity of the electrolyte, some valve grinding paste such as Richford's (coarse and fine), some jointing compound, a set of engine gaskets, some fine emery cloth, and a wire-brush type plug cleaner (*see* page 62).

The Sunbeam Tool Kit. The Sunbeam tool kit (*see* Figs. 27 and 28) is sufficient for all normal dismantling and assembling, and comprises a useful set of well finished tools. Some slight variations have been made since June, 1950, and earlier kits for the

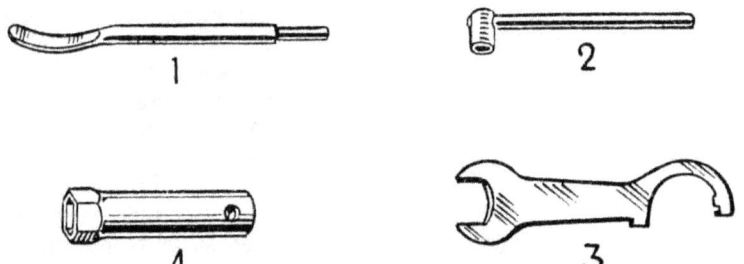

Fig. 28. Four Tools Supplied with Earlier Sunbeam Tool Kits (S7 and S8)

1. Combined tyre lever and tommy-bar (1946–50 S7 and S8) for use with item 4.
2. Small combined socket spanner and tommy-bar (1946–9 S7).
3. Spanner for handlebar mounting, front forks, and wheel bearing locking ring (1946–9 S7).
4. Box spanner for sparking plug (1946–50 S7 and S8).

S7 Sunbeam (with Sunbeam type front forks) have two spanners different to those used for later models. The variations are explained in the captions to the illustrations.

Additional Tools. The standard tool kit does not contain a feeler gauge for checking the sparking plug gap, and it is desirable to obtain a combined feeler gauge and plug gap regapping tool (*see* Fig. 32). An excellent tool is obtainable from the Champion Sparking Plug Co., Ltd. of Feltham, Middlesex, or from any Champion plug stockist. The pliers shown in Fig. 27 are not, of course, suitable for removing gudgeon-pin circlips, and a small pair of snipe-nosed pliers should be obtained from an accessory firm for this purpose. Another tool not included in the tool kit and needed for valve removal is a valve spring compressor. A special Sunbeam valve spring compressor is obtainable for a modest sum. Other Sunbeam special service tools (required for major overhauls) include a flywheel extractor, a spanner for the flywheel nut, a clutch assembly tool, and a front fork (S8) blade extractor and assembly tool.

It is desirable to purchase some good proprietary scrapers for decarbonizing the pistons and combustion chambers, though an old slightly blunted large screwdriver is fairly satisfactory for many purposes. Note that a scraper should be reasonably sharp because it is possible to inflict more damage on metal surfaces beneath carbon deposits by carelessly using a blunt tool than by using a sharp one with discretion.

If you decide to tackle as much work as possible in addition to routine adjustments, dismantling and assembling, you are advised to rig up a suitable bench, attach a vice to it, and buy a few extra tools. It is a good plan to begin by purchasing the following: a medium-weight hammer, a centre-punch, a hand-drill and an assortment of twist-drills, a hacksaw, some large and small files (rough and smooth), and a convenient soldering outfit for soldering nipples on to control cables. A good steel rule is also necessary. In this handbook space considerations do not permit of the author covering actual repair work, and unless you have had practical experience and have fair technical skill, you are not advised to tackle major repairs. It is often safer to entrust such work to the makers or to a reliable Sunbeam repair specialist.

Keep the Machine Clean. Proper cleaning of the machine and engine (internally and externally) is an essential part of general maintenance, and a necessary preliminary to stripping down. By paying regular attention to thorough cleaning you will not only keep your Sunbeam smart but also prevent any undue depreciation. Dirt often covers defects and can get inside the engine when it is being dismantled. Be careful not to permit dirt and grit to enter parts such as the carburettor, dynamo, hubs, brakes, etc. Also remember that mud and dirt accelerate rusting. After a ride in dirty weather cleaning the machine may take the best part of an hour. On no account leave a machine overnight in a wet condition. If you cannot spare the time for methodical cleaning during the winter months you should grease it lightly all over.

Clean the aluminium alloy and bright parts of the engine with rags and paraffin, assisted by suitable brushes where necessary. Scour off all filth from the engine sump and gearbox with a stiff brush and paraffin, and dry off with a clean rag. If the fins of the cylinder block and head become dirty, this reduces heat dispersion by radiation. Rub the fins with a stiff brush dipped in paraffin.

Never attempt to rub off mud when dry from the tank, frame, and mudguards, or the enamel lustre will quickly be spoiled. Use a hose or wipe over, using a sponge and pail of water. First soak the mud off and then float the mud off with copious supplies of

GENERAL MAINTENANCE AND OVERHAUL

clean water. When using a hose be very careful not to direct the stream of water on to the vital and vulnerable parts such as the carburettor, dynamo, distributor, hub bearings, etc. When all mud and dirt is removed, dry the enamelled parts with a chamois leather and afterwards polish the enamel with soft dusters and a good proprietary polish.

Cleaning the Chromium-plated Parts. Never clean any of the chromium-plated parts with metal polish or paste. Such cleaners contain oleic acid which attacks chromium. It is permissible, however, occasionally to clean the chromium with special chromium cleaning compound, though this is not really necessary. It is quite sufficient to clean the surfaces regularly with a damp chamois leather and afterwards polish them with a soft dry duster.

To reduce the tendency for tarnishing of the chromium to occur during the humid winter months, it is a good plan to smear the chromium with some "Tekall," obtainable in half-pint and pint tins from most accessory firms.

Check the Nuts for Tightness Regularly. On a new Sunbeam some preliminary bedding-down occurs and it is wise to check all external nuts and bolts for tightness fairly often. Pay special attention to the cylinder head nuts (see page 93). After completing the running-in period, check the nuts and bolts regularly about once a month. Most experienced motor-cyclists do this, and it can often save roadside trouble and damage.

ROUTINE MAINTENANCE

There are certain routine adjustments which should be checked at regular intervals and not left until an adjustment *has* to be made. This section deals with all those of importance.

Check the Valve Clearances Every 2,000 Miles. Every 2,000 miles and after decarbonizing and grinding-in the valves check the inlet and exhaust valve clearances, and if necessary adjust them. Actual adjustment is not often called for, except possibly during the running-in of a new or reconditioned engine.

The maintenance of correct valve clearances is absolutely essential for the maintenance of engine efficiency and high performance. Excessive clearances impose stresses, reduce power, and cause a most irritating noise. Insufficient clearances can cause serious damage to the valves (especially the exhaust valves) if the valves fail to close completely, and there is, of course, accompanying loss of compression and power. On all 1946 and subsequent Sunbeam engines the correct clearance for both inlet and exhaust valves *with the engine absolutely cold* is 0·018 in. (0·46 mm).

To Check the Valve Clearances. Place the Sunbeam on its central stand and remove the cylinder head cover after removing its three securing nuts. Now remove both sparking plugs and rotate the engine slowly until the valve whose clearance is to be checked is fully closed with its overhead inner rocker arm on the base circle (neutral portion) of the respective camshaft cam. To obtain this position for the inlet valve of the front cylinder, rotate the engine until the inlet valve of the rear cylinder is fully open. The two inlet valves just referred to are, of course, the second and third respectively from the front of the engine.

To ensure the rear inlet valve being fully closed, rotate the engine until the front inlet valve is fully open. Use the same

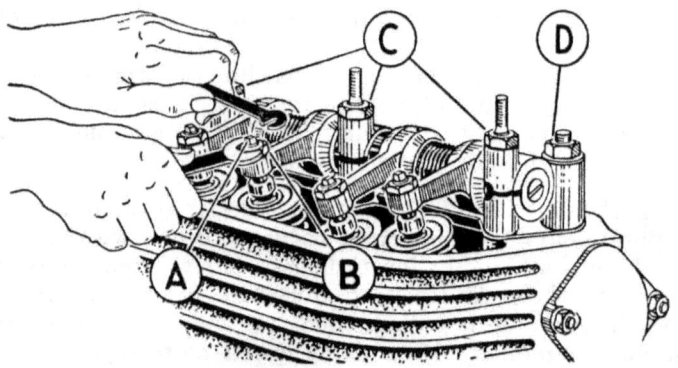

FIG. 29. ADJUSTING INLET VALVE CLEARANCE ON REAR CYLINDER

procedure for determining the fully closed position of the exhaust valves. Note that, considering the valves from the front to the rear of the engine, the exhaust valve of the front cylinder and of the rear cylinder are Nos. 1 and 4 respectively.

When a valve is fully closed, insert the 0·018 in. feeler gauge shown at 6 in Fig. 27 between the top of the valve stem and the pad of the rocker arm pin. If the valve clearance is correct, the feeler gauge should just enter without binding. If it refuses to enter or there is excessive play, adjust the valve clearance as described below.

To Adjust the Valve Clearances. If one or more of the four valve clearances are found to be incorrect, adjust (with the engine still *cold*) in the following manner. Referring to Fig. 29, hold each rocker arm pin *A* with the spanner shown at 5 in Fig. 27, and with the spanner shown at 3 slacken the pin lock-nut *B*. Then while holding the lock-nut *B*, screw the pin *A* into or out of the

GENERAL MAINTENANCE AND OVERHAUL

rocker arm end as required to obtain the 0·018 in. valve clearance. Having obtained this clearance, tighten the lock-nut *B* very securely while holding the rocker arm pin *A* with spanner 5. After tightening the lock-nut it is desirable again to check the valve clearance (*see* previous paragraph) in case the rocker arm pin should have turned slightly while tightening the lock-nut. Finally fit the cylinder head cover and secure with the three retaining nuts. Also replace the two sparking plugs, not forgetting their two copper washers.

Carburettor Maintenance. Instructions for tuning and cleaning the needle-jet Amal carburettor are given in Chapter II. For details of the standard carburettor settings for all 1946 and subsequent Sunbeams, *see* page 24.

Correct Lubrication. Detailed instructions on the correct lubrication of the Sunbeam engine and machine are given in Chapter III on pages 31 and 36 respectively. A useful lubrication chart is included on page 35.

Dynamo and Battery Maintenance. The care of the dynamo and battery, and also the lamps and horn, are discussed in detail in Chapter IV. The ignition components of the Lucas electrical equipment are dealt with later in this Chapter.

Suitable Sparking Plugs. To obtain full power output and avoid any tendency for pinking to occur, it is important always to run with suitable type sparking plugs fitted. Inferior plugs are quite unable to cope with the high temperatures prevailing in the Sunbeam combustion chambers. Sunbeam Motor Cycles, Ltd. fit Champion single-point non-detachable type N-5 plugs as standard, and one cannot go wrong by continuing to use this type of plug which has a 14 mm thread and a ¾ in. reach. Note that the Champion N-5 plug is suitable for hard driving, and when a machine is normally used for short trips only, it is better to fit a Champion type N-8 which is a hotter type and prevents oiling-up.

If you prefer to fit Lodge or K.L.G. sparking plugs, suitable types are the Lodge single-point non-detachable type HLN, and the K.L.G. detachable type FE70 or the watertight version, the K.L.G. WFE70 (*see* Fig. 30) with moulded terminal protector, steel sleeve for protecting insulation, heat dispersion fins, etc. For all-weather riding the use of a watertight plug or the fitting of a weatherproof terminal cover has much to commend it. A sectional view of the Lodge weatherproof terminal cover (negligible cost) is shown in Fig. 30 (left-hand sketch). It is also shock-proof and can be quickly fitted or detached. A convenient K.L.G.

weatherproof terminal cover which clips on to K.L.G. plugs and affords complete protection is also available.

Note that on all *new* machines registered for the first time after 1st July, 1953, it is obligatory to fit a sparking plug embodying an ignition suppressor, so as to prevent interference with radio and television receiver sets. This type of plug, by the way, facilitates starting-up from cold, and its electrodes last longer than do those

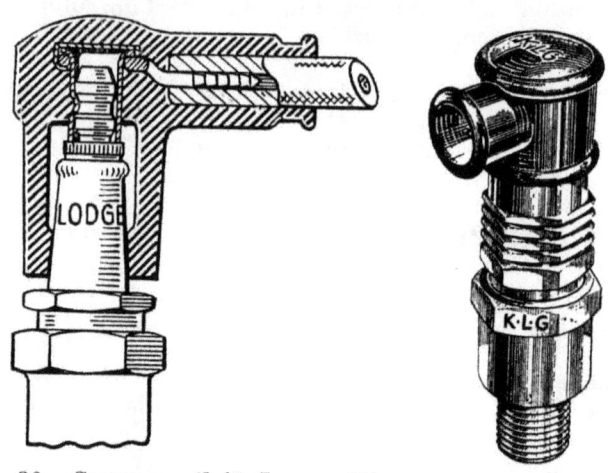

FIG. 30. SHOWING (*left*) LODGE WEATHERPROOF SPARKING PLUG TERMINAL COVER AND (*right*) K.L.G. WATERTIGHT PLUG

of the ordinary plug without an ignition suppressor. It is therefore recommended that all riders fit the modified-type plug as and when plug renewal becomes necessary.

The leading plug manufacturers now market excellent plugs with built-in suppressors and they also offer terminal covers of the waterproof type embodying ignition suppressors. These can be fitted to plugs of the non-suppressor type. Note that the ignition suppressor type K.L.G. plug has the letter "R" at the end of the type number (e.g., FE70R), and appropriate terminal covers are known as the "PS" and "SS" type.

Plug Trouble. Serious ignition trouble is rare, the commonest faults being sparking plug defects which can be remedied by cleaning and adjusting the plugs, or fitting new plugs when the old ones are clearly no longer fit for service. If the condition of a plug is so poor that *no* spark occurs, obviously the cylinder concerned will be cut right out, and extremely unbalanced running and poor starting will occur. If both plugs are unable to spark, the engine will clearly remain "dead." Should the condition of

GENERAL MAINTENANCE AND OVERHAUL

the plugs be such that only weak sparks occur, poor power output, misfiring, irregular slow-running, and poor starting will result.

If a sparking plug is thought to be at fault, remove it, with h.t. lead attached, and lay it on the cylinder head with its terminal clear of the head. Now rotate the engine sharply with the kick-starter and note if a good and regular spark occurs. It should be possible to hear a distinct click. If no spark or only a weak spark occurs and you get a "fat" spark at the distributor end, inspect and thoroughly overhaul the plug. It may be oiled-up, have heavy carbon or fuel deposits, burned electrodes, or have an incorrect gap between the points. It is also possible that the plug is worn out or has a damaged washer or insulation. All these possible faults should be checked. By making a regular inspection of both sparking plugs, plug trouble can be avoided.

Inspect Both Plugs Every 1,000 Miles. Regular inspection of both sparking plugs is desirable every 1,000 miles, when the plugs should be removed and carefully examined. If the carburettor is correctly tuned, there are no air leaks, no petrol leaks, and the strangler on the carburettor is used only when necessary (*see* page 10), the plug electrodes should remain clean for an almost indefinite period.

An excessively rich mixture will cause the electrode points to become sooty or carbonized very quickly and carbon deposits will also form inside the plug body within a short period. If carbon deposits form quickly, check your operation of the strangler. Even light deposits will have an adverse effect on engine performance. If you have been running on an anti-knocking fuel containing lead, you can expect grey coloured deposits to form somewhat rapidly. Oil getting past the piston rings into the combustion chambers will, of course, cause quick carbon formation, but remember that this fouling cannot occur unless the piston, rings, and cylinder are worn beyond the point at which a rebore is normally required. A faulty oil control ring, however, can cause over-lubrication and quick fouling of the piston and plug concerned. All carbon deposits must be very thoroughly cleaned off.

Quick Cleaning. If an inspection of each sparking plug shows it to be reasonably clean and not heavily carbonized, it is quite sufficient to clean it quickly by scraping the electrode points lightly with a sharp pocket-knife. A better method is to clean the points with a small piece of fine emery cloth. If this method is used, see that no abrasive particles are allowed to get inside the plug body. A good method of cleaning the inside of the plug body quickly is to use a proprietary plug cleaner, the usual type of which consists of a metal reservoir containing petrol and loose steel wires. Screw the sparking plug into the reservoir and then vigorously shake it. This removes all light carbon deposits. If no plug cleaner is available, use a fine wire brush. Heavy deposits necessitate thorough cleaning of the plugs.

Thorough Cleaning. Champion N-5, or N-8, and Lodge HLN plugs are all of the non-detachable type and cannot be dismantled for thorough cleaning, and when this is necessary take the plugs to a garage and have them thoroughly cleaned on a special plug cleaning machine such as the Champion service unit. Cleaning and testing takes only a few minutes. The plugs are cleaned of all deposits, washed, subjected to a high pressure air

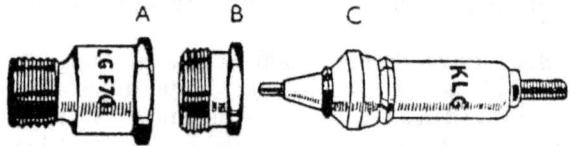

Fig. 31. Detachable Type Sparking Plug Dismantled for Thorough Cleaning

line, and afterwards tested for proper sparking at an air pressure of around 100 lb per sq. in.

With detachable type sparking plugs such as the K.L.G. FE70, it is advisable to dismantle the plugs for thorough cleaning in the event of the carbon deposits being heavy. Referring to Fig. 31, hold the hexagon *A* of the sparking plug body in a spanner or a vice. If the latter is used, take special care not to squeeze the hexagon between the jaws of the vice. With another spanner unscrew the gland nut *B*. It is now possible to detach the centre electrode *C*.

With a small knife scrape off all carbon deposits from the metal parts of the plug and afterwards rinse them in petrol. But do not scrape the insulation. If the insulation is covered with oil or soft carbon, wash it thoroughly with paraffin or petrol. Then with some fairly coarse emery cloth remove all carbon deposits and again wash in paraffin or petrol. With some fine emery cloth, polish the points of the electrodes, and re-assemble the sparking plug. See that no dirt or grit is lodged between the centre insulation and the plug body. Smear a little thin oil on the internal washer and verify that the washer seats correctly, otherwise a gas-tight seal may not be obtained. On no account over-tighten the gland nut, and verify that the copper washer (between the head and plug) is perfect. Before replacing the plugs, check the gap between the electrode points.

GENERAL MAINTENANCE AND OVERHAUL 63

Checking the Plug Gap. Under the influence of intense heat, chemical action, and continual sparking, the gap between the plug electrode points gradually but inevitably increases. Check the gap regularly with a suitable feeler gauge obtainable from accessory firms. The Champion Sparking Plug Co., Ltd.,

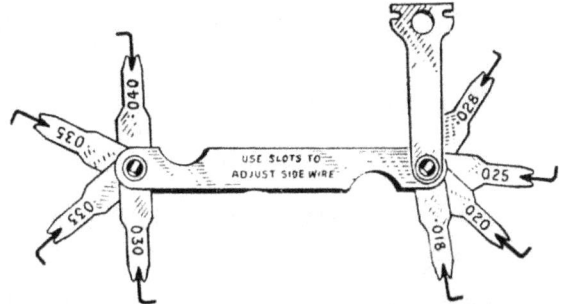

Fig. 32. Champion Combined Feeler Gauges and Plug Regapping Tool

Feltham, Middlesex, make an excellent combined set of special wire gauges and plug regapping tool (*see* Fig. 32). It can be obtained from any Champion plug stockist or from the makers, and though specially intended for Champion sparking plugs, is also suitable for regapping any make of plug. The correct gap for

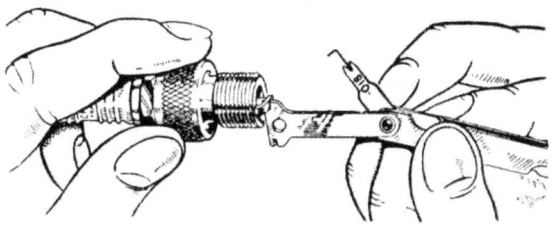

Fig. 33. Adjusting Gap of Champion Sparking Plug

Champion, Lodge, and K.L.G. plugs is 0·015 in. to 0·018 in. Obviously it is best when regapping a plug to adjust the points close to the lower limit. Further adjustment will not then be needed for a long time.

When regapping a sparking plug (after cleaning) always *press* the *outer* electrode(s). Never knock the outer electrode, and make no attempt to adjust the centre electrode. Fig. 33 illustrates the outer electrode of a Champion plug being pressed inwards with the slotted member of the Champion regapping tool shown in Fig. 32.

Replacing the Sparking Plugs. It is good practice to clean the threads on each plug body before replacing it in the cylinder head. Removal of carbon with a wire brush facilitates the fitting and removal of the plug and also improves heat dispersion (carbon is a bad heat conductor). Screw home both plugs by hand as far as possible and use the box spanner shown at 9 in Fig. 27 only for final tightening. Avoid using excessive force with the spanner because if the copper washer is unduly compressed it becomes hard and does not conduct heat so effectively. Some "blowing," however, may occur if the plugs are not screwed home sufficiently tightly. If the copper washers are not perfect, renew them. See that both h.t. leads are securely attached to the plug terminals.

Contact-breaker Adjustment. It is advisable to check and if necessary adjust the gap between the contacts of the contact-breaker on a new Sunbeam after covering 500 miles. Some bedding-down always occurs with a brand-new distributor unit. Subsequently it should not be necessary to check the gap more often than once every 6,000 miles. The functioning of the ignition system is adversely affected by an incorrect gap, and it should be noted that an excessive gap will advance the ignition timing. Always maintain the contact-breaker gap at 0·012 in.

To check the contact-breaker gap first remove the moulded distributor cap shown at 8 in Fig. 34. Now slowly rotate the engine until the contact-breaker contacts 3 are wide open. Then insert the (0·012 in.) feeler gauge attached to the Lucas screwdriver shown at 13 in Fig. 27 between the contacts. If the gap is correct, the feeler should be a sliding fit, no more and no less. If the gap varies appreciably from the gauge thickness, a contact-breaker adjustment is necessary. If cleaning is necessary, do this before making an adjustment.

To effect a contact-breaker adjustment, maintain the engine crankshaft position such that the contacts are wide open. Loosen the two screws 5 and 10 which secure the contact plate 11. Then move the plate as required until the gap between the contacts is precisely 0·012 in. Afterwards firmly retighten both locking screws and again check the gap.

To Clean the Distributor Unit. About every 6,000 miles remove the distributor cap (8 Fig. 34) and with a soft, dry cloth wipe the inside and outside absolutely clean, especially the space between the terminals. Inspect the contact-breaker. This, and especially the contacts 3, must never be allowed to get oily or dirty, or the contacts will become pitted or burned, and ignition trouble will develop. If both contacts have a grey frosted look, they probably require no attention. If they are only slightly discoloured, clean

GENERAL MAINTENANCE AND OVERHAUL

them with a petrol-moistened cloth. If the contacts are found to be burned or blackened, clean them thoroughly with a *fine* carborundum stone or, if not available, with some fine emery cloth. Do not remove more metal than is absolutely necessary. Then wipe away all dirt and metal dust with a petrol-moistened cloth.

Cleaning of the contacts is greatly facilitated by removing the contact-breaker rocker arm 1 which carries the moving contact.

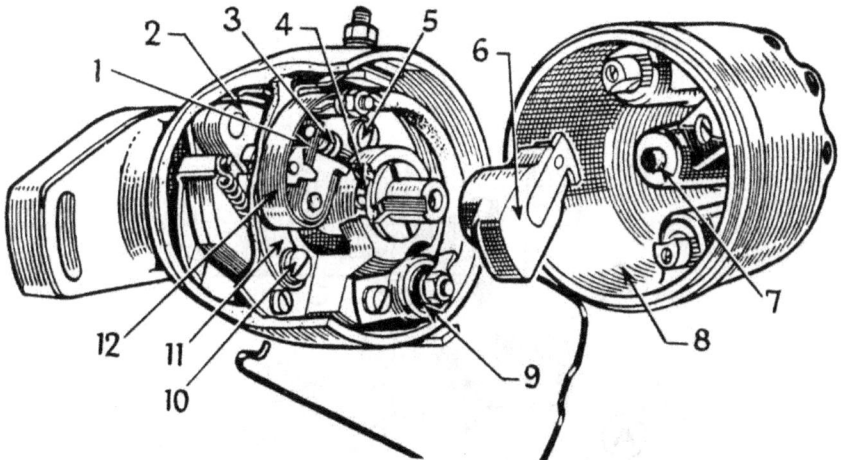

FIG. 34. THE LUCAS TYPE D1A2 DISTRIBUTOR UNIT

1. Contact-breaker rocker arm.
2. Automatic ignition timing unit.
3. Contacts of contact-breaker.
4. Ball bearing.
5. Screw securing contact plate.
6. Rotor.
7. Carbon brush.
8. Distributor cap.
9. Condenser.
10. Screw securing contact plate.
11. Contact plate.
12. Contact-breaker spring.

To remove the arm, unscrew the nut securing the end of its spring 12, remove the spring washer, and flat washer, and withdraw the arm, complete with spring. After cleaning the contacts, always make a point of checking the gap between them with the contacts fully open.

Check the Timing Chain Tension Every 2,000 Miles.
With the engine quite *cold*, rotate it until one exhaust valve (it does not matter which) commences to open. This causes the camshaft driving chain to become slack on the chain tensioner side. Referring to Fig. 35, remove the cover which is secured by the two screws *A*. Then loosen the pinch-bolt *B*. The effect of doing this is to allow the spring tensioner to bear correctly against the slack chain run. Afterwards tighten the pinch-bolt, replace the cover, and tighten the two securing screws *A*. When replacing

the cover do not forget to replace its fibre washer and the two fibre washers provided for the cover securing screws. Note that on S7 engines prior to September, 1948, a non-adjustable tensioner (*see* Fig. 62) is fitted.

Verify the Engine Damper Clearances Every 1,000 Miles. Referring to Fig. 36, two engine damper snubbers are located, one

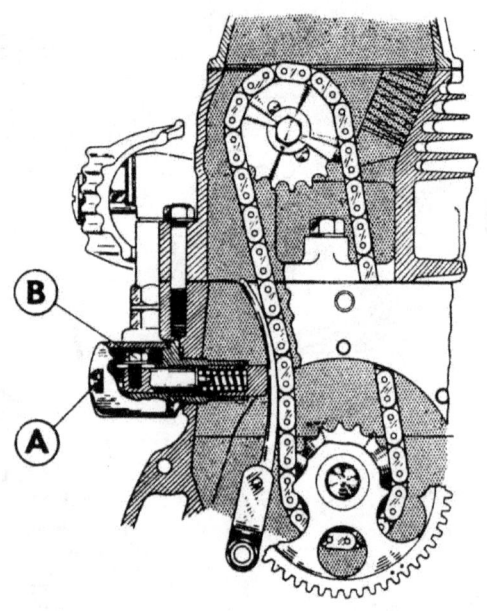

Fig. 35. Adjustable Spring Tensioner for Camshaft Driving Chain

A non-adjustable type (*see* Fig. 62) was used prior to September, 1948

on each side of the front frame member D. They operate against two fibre stops screwed to the crankcase. It is important, if maximum efficiency is to be obtained, to verify the clearance between each snubber and its corresponding fibre stop. The correct clearance, which should be checked by means of a feeler gauge (with the engine in its static position) is 0·015 in–0·020 in.

To Adjust the Engine Damper Clearances. Slacken each snubber lock-nut and turn the snubber until a clearance of 0·015 in.–0·020 in. is obtained, and afterwards retighten the lock-nut.

Referring to Fig. 67, the snubber plate G (shown also at C in Fig. 36) at the top rear of the engine also carries two horizontally-opposed torque reaction members, snubbers N. Shims can be

GENERAL MAINTENANCE AND OVERHAUL 67

inserted behind the snubbers to compensate for excessive wear on the rubber faces, and it is important to maintain the clearances between each torque reaction damper and the central tongue A at 0·015 in.–0·020 in. (with the engine in the static position).

Referring to Fig. 67, to be sure that both bottom and top damper snubbers are properly synchronized, and that the distance piece through the damper plate D remains in the centre of the

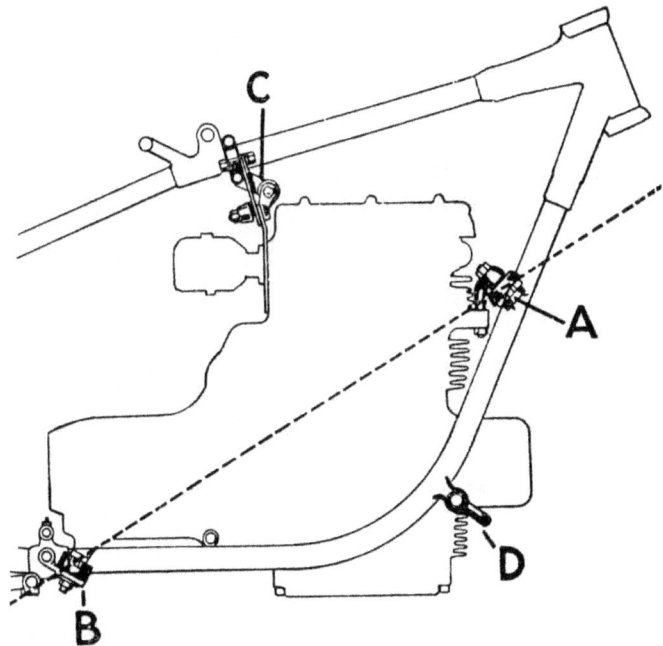

FIG. 36. DIAGRAM SHOWING LOCATION OF ENGINE DAMPER SNUBBERS (1949 ONWARDS)

For details of snubber assembly at C, refer to Fig. 67

elongated slot, first loosen the nuts on the two bolts E. Slacken the frame clip bracket O by undoing the nut on the *upper* bolt B. Now centralize the clip bracket O so that the tongue A is halfway between the snubbers N, and the point of maximum movement (0·030 in.–0·040 in.) is taken up simultaneously on both bottom and top snubbers. The upper near-side and the lower off-side snubbers should touch simultaneously, and vice versa. Finally tilt the power unit in each direction and carefully check the engine damper clearances with a feeler gauge. Be sure that the tongue A is locked in the frame clip bracket O. Then verify that the nut of the upper bolt B clamping the clip bracket to the frame top tube is firmly tightened. Also check for tightness the two damper plate-securing nuts on the bolts *E*.

Tyre Maintenance. To get the maximum mileage from the tyre covers and tubes, you should drive with care and pay regular attention to the proper maintenance of the tyres. Do not indulge unnecessarily in crash braking, fierce acceleration, and cornering at a sharp angle. Riding moderately will save much tread wear and will probably "get you there" just as quickly. Do not allow the tyres to rest in a welter of oil or paraffin, and, if it gets on the tyres, clean the treads with some petrol. Never leave the machine for long without its being jacked up on its centre stand. Fre-

FIG. 37. A CONVENIENT TYRE PRESSURE GAUGE—
THE DUNLOP PENCIL-TYPE NO. 6

quently spin the wheels and scrutinize the covers for flints and small stones which may have become embedded in the treads. Remove all such potential sources of punctures immediately.

Check the Tyre Pressures Weekly. It is advisable to check the tyre pressures weekly with a suitable pressure gauge such as the Dunlop No. 6 (*see* Fig. 37), the Romac, the Schrader No. 7750, or the Holdtite gauge. If the inflation pressures are found to be above or below those recommended, pump up or deflate the tyres until the pressures *are* correct. It just is not good enough to kick the tyres as riders were apt to do in the past. Good tyre mileage, freedom from skidding, and maximum comfort depend in no small degree upon the pressures being maintained correct. Slight air leakage sometimes occurs at the valves, and therefore make a practice of keeping the valve caps screwed on tightly. If you ride solo and your weight does not exceed 140 lb (10 stone) you are advised to keep your tyres inflated in accordance with the pressures given in Table I. If your weight exceeds 140 lb, or you carry a pillion passenger or heavy luggage, you should inflate the tyres (except 4·50–16 and 4·75–16) in accordance with the Dunlop minimum inflation pressures given in Table II. In this instance you should take or ride the Sunbeam to the nearest weighbridge and check individually the fully-laden weight on the front and rear tyres. Then consult Table II for the front and rear correct minimum inflation pressures. Most large railway stations and transport depots include a suitable weighbridge.

GENERAL MAINTENANCE AND OVERHAUL 69

Models S7 and S8 have an unladen weight (dry) of 430 lb and 405 lb, respectively.

TABLE I

TYRE SIZES AND INFLATION PRESSURES FOR SOLO RIDING

Tyre	Models S7 and S7 de luxe	Model S8
Sizes—		
Front tyre	4·50–16	3·25–19
Rear tyre	4·75–16	4·00–18
Sidecar tyre	3·50–19	3·50–19
Pressures (lb per sq. in.)–		
Front (solo)	19	18
Rear (solo)	19	16
Front (sidecar)	19	24
Rear (sidecar)	19	16
Sidecar	16	16

TABLE II

DUNLOP TYRE MINIMUM INFLATION PRESSURES
(Showing load per tyre in lb, and recommended pressures in lb per sq. in.)

Pressures	16	18	20	24	28	32
Tyre size	Load per tyre (fully laden)					
3·25–19	200	240	280	350	400	440
3·50–19	280	320	350	400	450	500
4·00–18	360	400	430	500	—	—

Note that Table II does not include minimum inflation pressures for the 4·50–16 Dunlop ribbed front tyre and the 4·75–16 Dunlop "Universal" rear tyre provided on Models S7 and S7 de luxe. The Service Department of The Dunlop Rubber Co., Ltd. recommend the following inflation pressures where a rider weighs over 10 stone—
1. If rider's weight is 12 stone, give 20 lb per sq. in. front and rear.
2. If rider's weight is 12 stone, plus 50 lb luggage in panniers, give 20 lb per sq. in. front, and 22 lb per sq. in. rear.
3. If rider's weight is 12 stone, plus a pillion rider of the same weight, give 21 lb per sq. in. front, and 28 lb per sq. in. rear.

Saddle Adjustment (Model S7 Only). On the 1949–57 Model S8 the saddle has the usual three-point mounting as provided on most other motor-cycles. On the 1946–9 Model S7 and the 1949–57 Model S7 de luxe, however, the saddle has a spring suspension which can be adjusted to suit the rider's weight. Referring to Fig. 38, the lower frame has three holes, and the bolt is illustrated engaged in the centre hole which is intended for

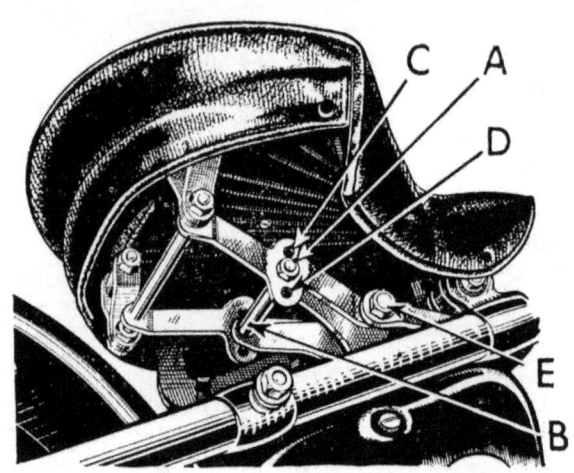

FIG. 38. MODEL S7 DE LUXE SADDLE SUSPENSION
Applicable to 1949 and subsequent models. For details of the saddle suspension on 1946–9 Model S7 (with Sunbeam-type forks), see Fig. 18

riders weighing ten stone. Holes *C* and *D* are for riders whose weight is more or less than ten stone, respectively.

To alter the saddle position, with a suitable spanner remove nut *A* and tap out the bolt. Then swing the cradle *B* as required up or down until it is aligned with hole *C* or *D*, according to which is to be used. Afterwards replace the bolt and tighten nut *A* securely.

Sidecar "Toe-in." Where a sidecar is attached it is important, to ensure minimum tyre wear and maximum stability, that the sidecar has the right amount of "toe-in." Where a Sunbeam sidecar (*see* Fig. 3) is attached, the correct "toe-in" is automatically assured, because there is no adjustment for the sidecar attachment arms, all dimensions being pre-determined and fixed. Alignment of the sidecar wheel relatively to the motor-cycle wheels therefore must always remain correct, and the same applies to the vertical alignment of the motor-cycle itself. As regards the motor-cycle wheels, since shaft drive is provided

GENERAL MAINTENANCE AND OVERHAUL 71

instead of a secondary chain, the design does not allow for movement of the rear wheel in the frame, and the two wheels therefore always remain dead parallel to each other.

Front and Rear Wheel Bearings. Ball and roller journal bearings of the type shown in Fig. 39 are provided for the front and rear hubs of all 1946 and subsequent Sunbeam models, with the

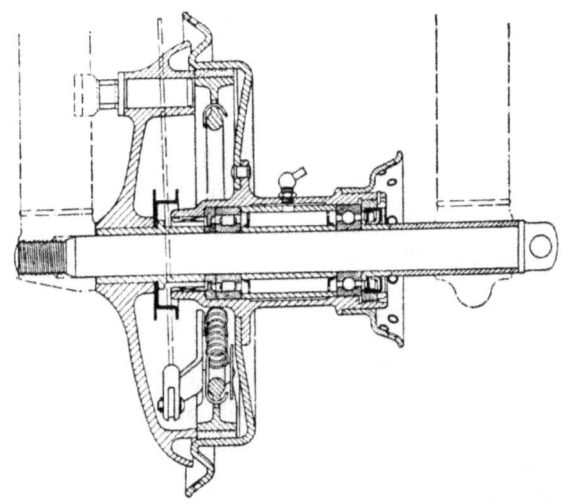

FIG. 39. BALL AND ROLLER JOURNAL BEARING HUB
Applicable to all hubs except the front one on Model S8

exception of the front hub of Model S8 which has two ball bearings as illustrated in Fig. 40. All hub bearings are non-adjustable and require no attention other than lubrication, which is dealt with on page 36. Dismantling of the hubs is normally never required, but should a ball or roller disintegrate or other damage occur (rare) the hubs can readily be dismantled and assembled if careful note is taken of their construction, which is clearly shown in the two accompanying sectional drawings.

To Remove the Front or Rear Wheel (Models S7, S7 de Luxe).
On all 1946 and subsequent S7 type machines the wheels are instantly detachable and interchangeable. Both hubs have "knock-out" spindles, and, if a puncture occurs, wheel removal can be very readily effected in the following manner.

First raise the wheel concerned clear of the ground by using the appropriate stand. Then, referring to Figs. 41 and 42, loosen the pinch-bolt A. Next insert a tommy-bar B through the hole at the end of the detachable wheel spindle, unscrew the spindle (clockwise), and draw it right out. Note particularly that in the case of both front and rear hubs the spindle has a *left-hand thread*

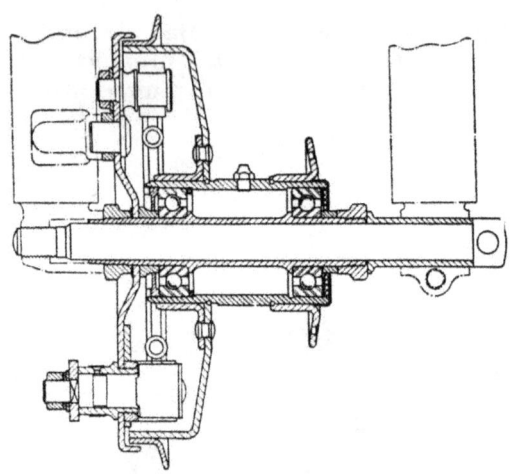

Fig. 40. Ball Bearing Front Hub
Used only on Model S8

and no attempt should be made to unscrew it in the usual anti-clockwise direction.

Having removed the detachable spindle, ease the wheel sideways to the near side to enable the brake drum to clear the

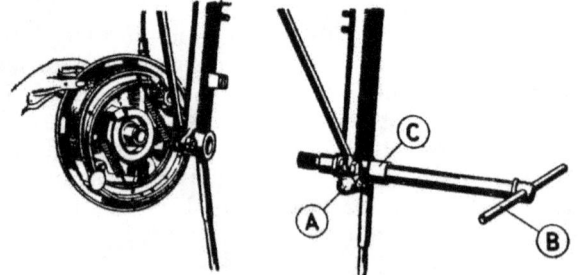

Fig. 41. Front Wheel Removal (S7)

internal expanding shoes. The wheel will then slide out and can be lifted away from the machine. Observe that when the wheel is eased sideways to let the drum clear the shoes, the distance bush *C* (Figs. 41 and 42) slides into the wheel bracket and should be left there prior to replacement of the wheel.

GENERAL MAINTENANCE AND OVERHAUL 73

Replacing the Front or Rear Wheel (Models S7, S7 de Luxe).
This is perfectly straightforward. Note that the distance bush C (Figs. 41 and 42) will take up its correct location in the fork end if the forks are depressed once or twice. Correct positioning of the bush is essential to proper fork alignment and functioning. There is also one other *very* important point to watch. Make quite sure that the detachable spindle is screwed home anti-clockwise absolutely tightly *before* you re-tighten the pinch-bolt A.

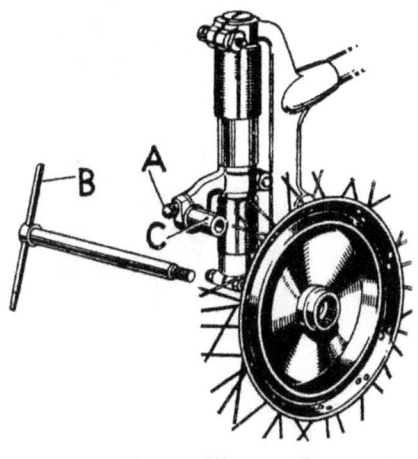

Fig. 42. REAR WHEEL REMOVAL (S7 AND S8)

To Remove the Front or Rear Wheel (Model S8). Referring to Figs 42 and 43, follow the instructions already given for Models S7 and S7 de luxe. Prior to removing the front wheel you must first disconnect the front brake cable. The rear hub design is identical on all Sunbeam models, but in the case of Model S8 although the front and rear wheels are instantly detachable, they are not interchangeable as on Models S7 and S7 de luxe. Some details of the front hub mounting on Model S8 are illustrated in Fig. 43.

To Replace the Front or Rear Wheel (Model S8). This is done exactly as in the case of the wheels of Models S7 or S7 de luxe. Where the front or rear hub is concerned, you should refer to Fig. 43 or 42, respectively. Do not forget that the wheels are *not* interchangeable. Check that the front brake cable is properly re-connected and adjusted.

Check the Steering Head Adjustment Every 1,000 Miles.
Although it is desirable to check the adjustment every 1,000 miles, actual adjustment is not often called for. Jack up the front of the machine by placing a box or other suitable packing beneath the engine sump, so that the front wheel is clear of the ground. Also slacken the steering damper right off. Then stand in front of the Sunbeam astride its front wheel, grasp the telescopic fork shrouds, and attempt to move the shrouds up and down (*see* Fig. 44). If the steering head adjustment is correct, it should be possible to turn the handlebars and forks quite freely without feeling any perceptible end play when attempting to move the

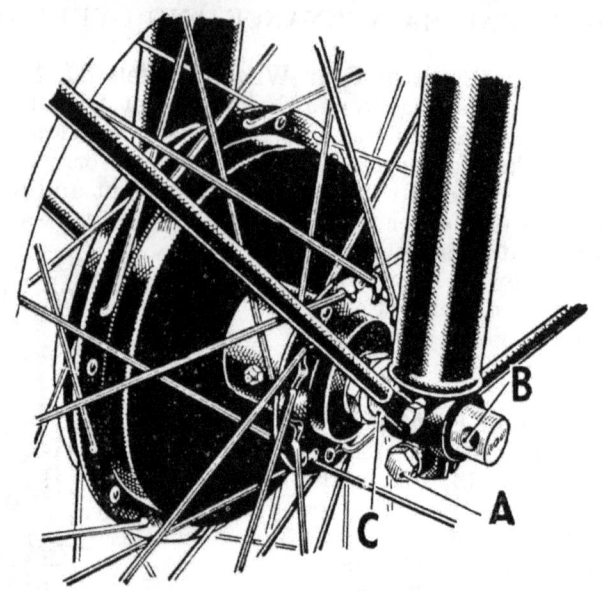

Fig. 43. Front Wheel Removal (S8)

Key to Figs. 41–43

A. Pinch bolt.   *B*. Tommy-bar.   *C*. Distance bush

Fig. 44. Testing for Play in Steering Head

GENERAL MAINTENANCE AND OVERHAUL 75

fork shrouds. If perceptible play is present, adjust the steering head as required in accordance with the instructions which follow.

To Adjust the Steering Head (B.S.A. type Forks). The following instructions apply to the 1949–57 Models S8 and S7 de luxe

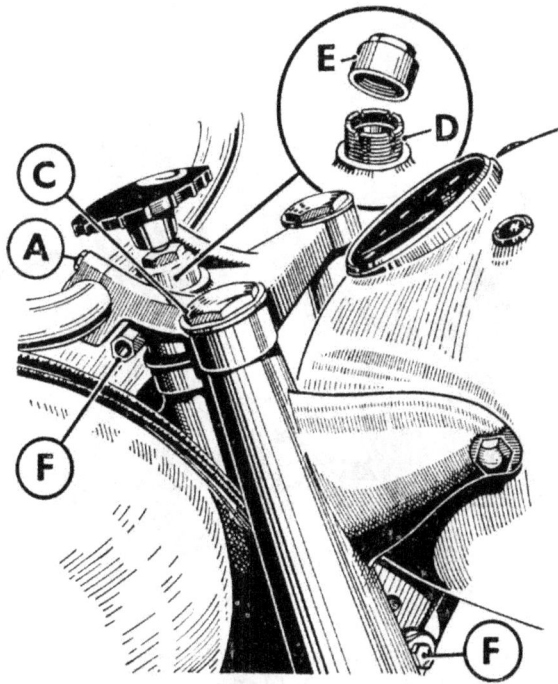

FIG. 45. STEERING HEAD ADJUSTMENT
(1949–57 Model S8)

with B.S.A. type front forks. Reference should be made to Figs. 45 and 46, respectively.

With the front wheel clear of the ground, unscrew the steering damper knob (with stem), and remove this, followed by the steering head lock-nut E. Also loosen the three pinch-bolts F. Then tighten the adjuster sleeve D (clockwise) until all end play has been eliminated. It is important not to over-tighten the adjuster sleeve, otherwise stiffness of the steering will occur and the ball races may become damaged. If you find that you have over-tightened the adjuster sleeve D, slacken it off (anti-clockwise) a shade. After making a steering head adjustment, re-tighten the three pinch-bolts F and the steering head lock-nut

E. Also fit the steering damper knob (with stem), but before screwing home the damper, again check the adjustment of the steering head as already described. When the adjustment is

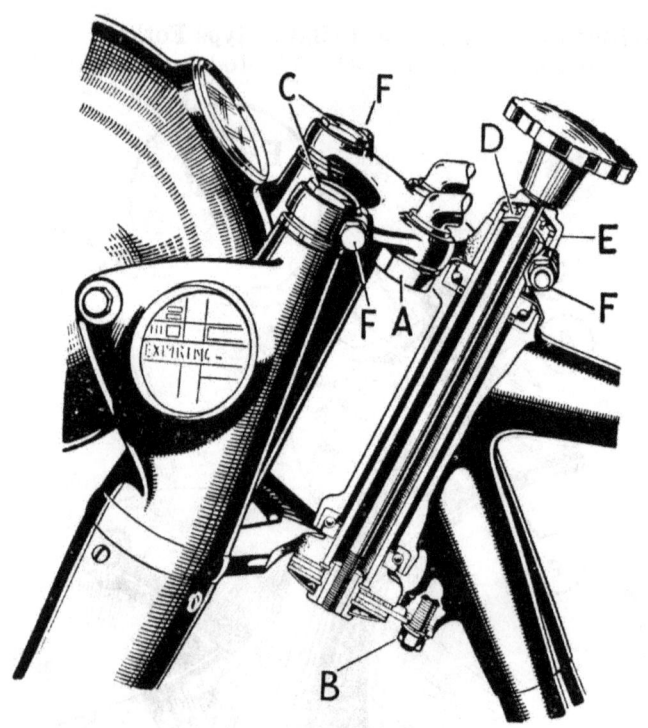

Fig. 46. Steering Head Adjustment
(1949-57 Model S7 de-luxe)

confirmed to be correct, remove the packing from beneath the engine sump.

To Adjust the Steering Head (Sunbeam type Forks). The steering head adjustment on the 1946-9 Model S7 with Sunbeam type telescopic front forks is illustrated in Fig. 47. To make an adjustment (with front wheel raised clear of the ground), slacken the three pinch-bolts *F* and with the appropriate spanner applied to the adjuster *E*, screw the adjuster up or down as required until all end play in the steering head bearings is eliminated and the handlebars and front forks turn readily. Afterwards tighten the three pinch-bolts firmly, again check the adjustment, and, if correct, remove the packing from below the engine sump.

GENERAL MAINTENANCE AND OVERHAUL 77

Check the Clutch Adjustment Every 1,000 Miles. The clutch, which is of car-type, has one substantial friction plate (*see* Fig. 76) which wears very gradually unless wear is accelerated by using

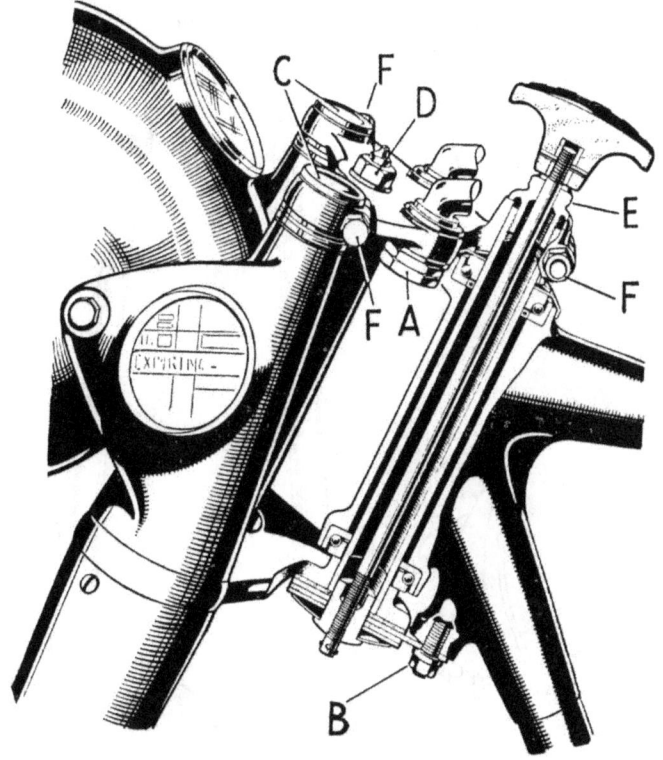

FIG. 47. STEERING HEAD ADJUSTMENT
(1946-9 Model S7)

the clutch carelessly and, particularly, by permitting unnecessary slipping. The range of clutch movement provided by the makers is such that small clutch adjustments at short intervals are neither necessary nor allowed for. Nevertheless it is advisable to make a quick inspection of the clutch adjustment about every 1,000 miles.

There must always be a little free movement (about $\frac{1}{32}$ in. to $\frac{1}{16}$ in.) in the clutch-operating mechanism when the clutch is fully engaged. This, of course, applies to all clutches on all motorcycles. On Sunbeam models, as wear of the friction linings very slowly occurs, the free movement in the operating mechanism decreases, and after some thousands of miles may eventually disappear completely, unless regular adjustment is made. Always maintain the small amount of free movement by making the necessary adjustments as required by means of the adjuster on the clutch cable. When, however, the free movement is reduced by friction plate wear to a mere few thousandths of an inch, and no further effective cable adjustment can be made, it is necessary to have the friction plate relined (*see also* next paragraph) and

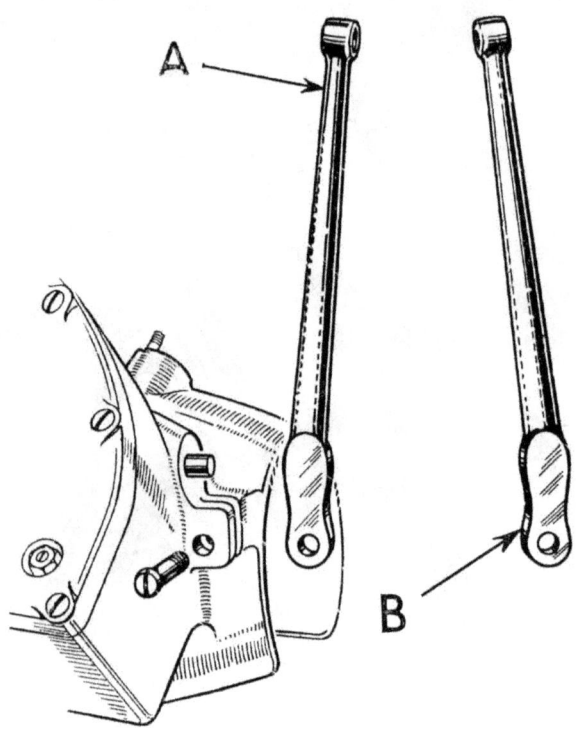

FIG. 48. ALTERNATIVE POSITIONS OF CLUTCH OPERATING LEVERS
A. Normal position of lever. *B*. Lever reversed to compensate for clutch wear. The lever is not reversible from March, 1950, onwards

then make the necessary cable adjustment. The clutch spring pressure is *not* adjustable.

Operating Lever Reversible (Some Models). On all Sunbeams up to the end of February, 1950, it is possible to reverse the clutch-operating lever to restore free movement in the clutch-operating mechanism when friction lining wear reduces (in spite of cable adjustments) free movement to a few thousandths of an inch. The normal position of the lever is shown at *A* in Fig. 48 and the

GENERAL MAINTENANCE AND OVERHAUL 79

reversed position at B. On most 1950 and all subsequent models this form of adjustment is omitted, as it is considered by the makers to be no longer necessary.

Kick-starter Ratchet Adjustment (Model S7). On Model S7 Sunbeams up to September, 1947, a ratchet adjustment is provided for the kick-starter (omitted on all subsequent models).

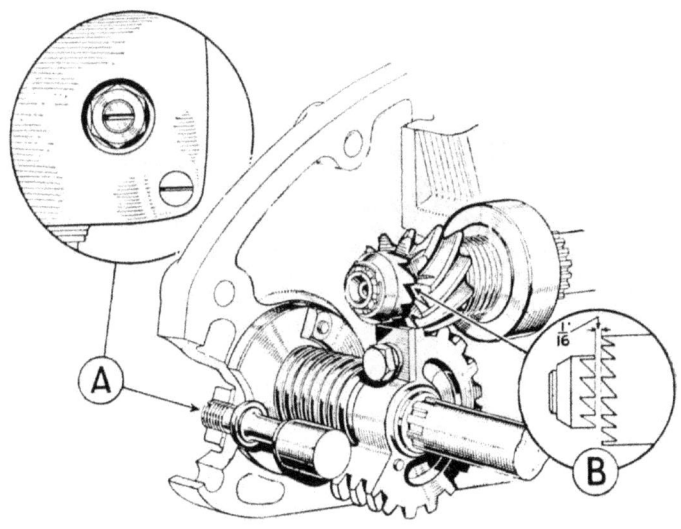

FIG. 49. KICK-STARTER RATCHET ADJUSTMENT (MODEL S7)
This adjustment was deleted in September, 1947

Referring to Fig. 49, the kick-starter mechanism includes right-angle skew gears, and it is most important to keep these skew gears correctly adjusted, so that a full kick-starter stroke may be obtained, with a clearance between the kick-starter ratchet pinion and the ratchet itself in the non-operative position. A faulty adjustment causes the ratchet to be in continual engagement, and this causes undue wear and noise. An adjustment is provided at the kick-starter quadrant stop shown at A in Fig. 49. It is eccentrically mounted.

To make a kick-starter adjustment, allow the engine to idle slowly in neutral, and loosen the lock-nut on the stop spindle. The lock-nut is the lower hexagon at the rear on the near-side cover plate on the gearbox. Now with a screwdriver turn the spindle clockwise or anti-clockwise as required until the ratchet teeth just touch. It is easy to identify this position because of the "ratchety" noise which occurs. Then turn the spindle back immediately about a third of a turn and tighten the lock-nut.

The mechanism will assume the position illustrated at *B* in Fig. 49, where the clearance between the tips of the two sets of ratchet teeth is about one-sixteenth of an inch.

To Adjust the Front Brake (Model S7 and S7 de Luxe). On the 1946–9 Model S7 and the 1949 and later Model S7 de luxe, when an adjustment is required to compensate for cable stretch and/or wear of the brake shoe linings, it is not necessary to interfere with the operating cable. The adjustment is provided at the brake shoe fulcrum, and it should be made with the wheel raised clear of the ground. Referring to Fig. 50, with a spanner applied to the square head on the brake adjuster, turn the adjuster in a *clockwise* direction as indicated at Fig. 50. When the adjuster turns it emits a series of "clicks," each "click" being equivalent to a quarter of a turn. To adjust the front brake correctly, turn the square-headed adjuster clockwise as far as it will go. Then slacken off the adjuster one "click."

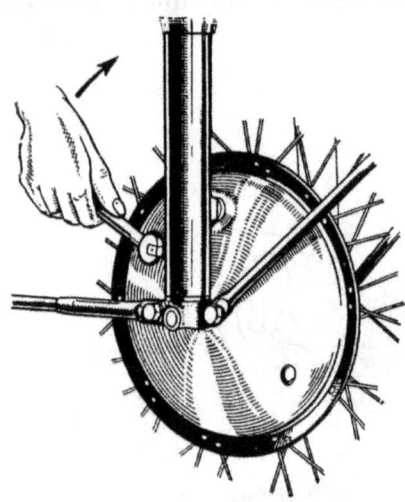

FIG. 50. ADJUSTING FRONT BRAKE

Applies to Models S7 and S7 de luxe

The above setting ensures maximum efficiency, with the shoes just clear of the brake drum when the brake is not applied, and close enough to give instant control when the brake lever is used.

Adjusting the Front Brake (Model S8). On the 1949 and later Model S8, to adjust the front brake, first raise the front wheel clear of the ground and then make the necessary adjustment with the knurled thumb nut and lock-nut located on the cable stop at the lower end of the front fork leg.

Having adjusted the front brake so that there is plenty of leverage at the handlebar control without any tendency for the brake shoes to bind on the brake drum when the wheel is spun by hand, proceed to centralize the shoe assembly. Loosen the large nut on the brake cover plate so as to slacken the fulcrum pin in its slotted hole. Then operate the front brake lever, when the fulcrum pin will automatically centralize the assembly. Finally with the brake still firmly applied, tighten the large nut on the brake cover plate.

GENERAL MAINTENANCE AND OVERHAUL 81

To Adjust the Rear Brake (Models S7, S7 de Luxe, and S8).
Instructions for doing this on the 1946–9 Model S7 and the 1949 and subsequent Models S7 de luxe and S8 are identical to those

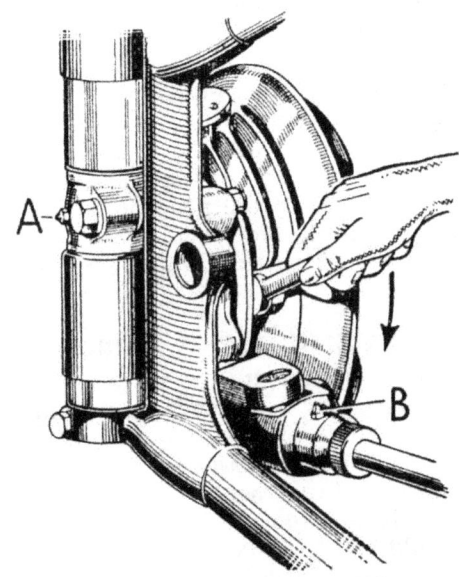

FIG. 51. ADJUSTING REAR BRAKE
Applies to Models S7, S7 de luxe, and S8
A. Grease nipple for rear springing.
B. Grease nipple for rear universal joint.

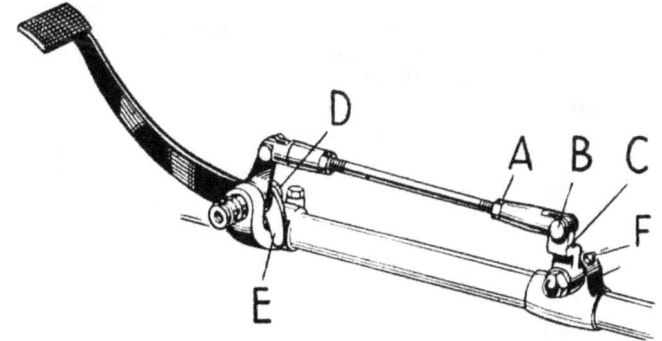

FIG. 52. REAR BRAKE PEDAL ADJUSTMENT
Applies to all models

already given for the front brake of Models S7 and S7 de luxe (*see* page 80). Fig. 51 shows a spanner being applied in a clockwise direction to the square head of the rear brake adjuster.

Adjusting the Rear Brake Pedal. The rear brake pedal on all Sunbeams can conveniently be adjusted for height to suit the physical characteristics of individual riders. The adjustment is entirely independent of the control cable adjustment already dealt with. Referring to Fig. 52, if a pedal adjustment is needed, first loosen the lock-nut A and also the brake pedal nut D. Next remove the split-pin from the toggle pin B, and take out the pin. Then lift the toggle quite clear of the lever C and screw it in or out as required until you obtain the pedal position which suits you best when the toggle is reconnected to the lever C. When you have obtained the best pedal position, replace the toggle pin split-pin, press back the brake lever stop plate E hard against the lug, and finally re-tighten the brake pedal nut D and also the toggle lock-nut A.

DECARBONIZING, VALVE GRINDING, ETC.

After a considerable mileage it is desirable to undertake a top overhaul, which comprises decarbonizing, grinding-in the valves, and a careful inspection of the valve springs, camshaft, etc. Periodical decarbonizing is essential to the maintenance of engine efficiency, but it is not necessary to decarbonize regularly at fixed intervals. This maintenance operation (and the grinding-in of the valves) should be undertaken only *when it becomes necessary*.

It is almost impossible not to become aware that the engine needs to be "decoked." Its normal smooth running and high performance gradually deteriorate; a tendency to "pink" and "knock," especially when accelerating or hill climbing, develops; gone is that youthful liveliness and surging power; the exhaust sounds noticeably "woolly"; slow-running becomes rather uncertain; flexibility suffers; and in extreme instances there may be some over-heating. If the foregoing unpleasant symptoms are accompanied by poor compression (as tested with the kick-starter), it is practically certain that the valves require to be ground-in, assuming that the piston rings have not become badly worn. Note that pinking is on rare occasions caused by sticking of the automatic ignition-advance mechanism.

Valve deterioration (caused mainly by oxidation of the seatings) generally coincides with the formation of carbon deposits in the engine, and it is therefore advisable to inspect the valves and valve seats each time you decarbonize. Grind-in the valves only if a careful inspection shows this to be *necessary*.

Preliminary Stripping Down. Dismantling for decarbonizing is facilitated by removing the petrol tank, and this should always be done. Note that the tank is insulated from the frame top tube by two rubber cushions which must always be replaced

GENERAL MAINTENANCE AND OVERHAUL 83

in their original positions. Before you disturb the petrol tank, first turn off the petrol. If you have been running on the reserve fuel supply, turn off *both* petrol taps. Now disconnect the petrol pipe union beneath the float chamber of the carburettor. Remove the air cleaner cover by unscrewing its securing screws (three provided on most engines), and proceed to remove the Amal carburettor from the engine. Unscrew the mixing chamber lock ring Z (Fig. 7) and withdraw the throttle slide and strangler slide (where fitted). Tie up the slide(s) in a convenient, safe position

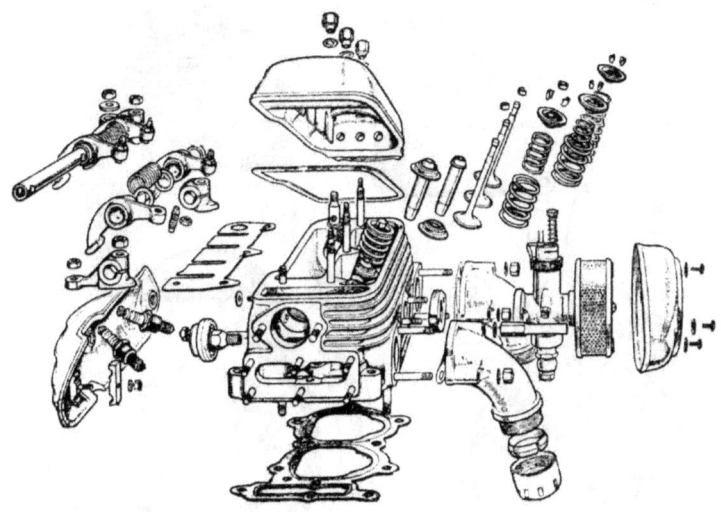

FIG. 53. EXPLODED VIEW OF CYLINDER HEAD, OVERHEAD VALVE GEAR, ETC.
(*From "Motor Cycle," London*)

to facilitate further dismantling. Then remove the two carburettor flange securing nuts and withdraw the carburettor, together with the distance washer between its flange and the engine.

Detach both exhaust pipes by removing the two nuts which secure each exhaust pipe flange to the corresponding exhaust port. Observe that on Models S7 de luxe and S8 the front nut on the exhaust pipe rear flange is extended to receive the rear screw for the air cleaner cover. Take off the bracket holding the exhaust pipes to the gearbox, and also the clip and bolt located at the front and rear respectively of each silencer. You can now swing the entire exhaust system well clear of the engine.

Removing the Cylinder Head. After stripping down the various components as already described, remove the distributor cap

(8, Fig. 34), disconnect the low tension lead at the side of the distributor unit, and detach the plug cover by unscrewing the two knurled nuts. Also remove the connexion from the oil pressure indicator unit and disconnect the high tension leads from the two sparking plugs. Take out both plugs, being careful not to lose their copper washers. Now take off the cylinder head

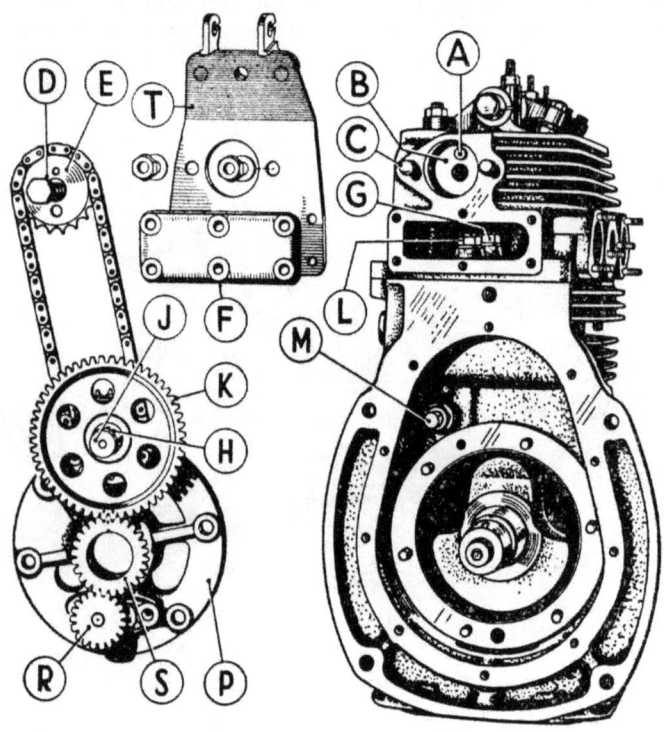

FIG. 54. DIAGRAM SHOWING CAMSHAFT DRIVE AT REAR OF ENGINE, ETC.
The nut L was omitted prior to March, 1949

cover, secured by three nuts (*see* Fig. 53) and withdraw the cover. Should the joint be somewhat stiff, apply a few *light* taps with a wooden mallet to free the joint. Undo the nuts from the two studs shown at C in Fig. 54 and remove the distributor unit.

Referring to Fig. 54, rotate the engine (in neutral) with the kick-starter, or alternatively (and preferably) by engaging fourth gear and turning the rear wheel slowly by hand until the pistons are at top dead centre and the hole in the camshaft sprocket, for the distributor driving peg, is positioned vertically below the camshaft centre. Positioned thus, the driving peg hole A on the

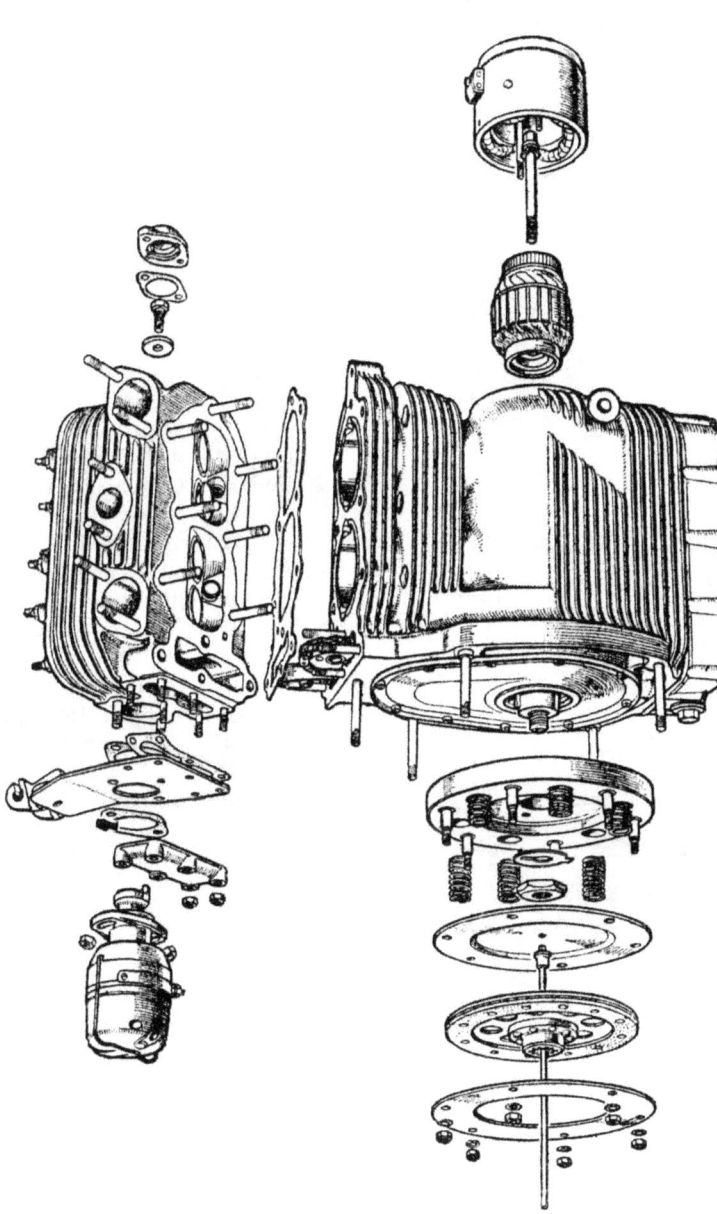

Fig. 55. Exploded View of Engine with Cylinder Head, Clutch, etc., Withdrawn
(*From "The Motor Cycle," London*)

flange *B* at the driving end of the camshaft is located vertically above the centre of the camshaft as illustrated in Fig. 54. Now unscrew bolt *D* and withdraw the camshaft sprocket *E*.

Unscrew evenly in the order shown in Fig. 61 the eleven nuts which secure the cylinder head block to the cylinder block (the studs themselves are on the head). The eleven securing nuts comprise: one at the front; one at the rear; three along each side; and three extra nuts and bolts at the rear. These extra nuts and bolts are designed to seal the joint face at the camshaft driving chain tunnel at the rear of the cylinder block. Do not forget to remove the nuts shown at *G* and *L* in Fig. 54. Until the snubber plate *G* (Fig. 67) and the cover plate *F* (Fig. 54) are detached these two nuts are not visible or accessible. Having removed all the nuts and bolts securing the cylinder head, lift the cylinder head block off the cylinder block. Remove the cylinder head gasket (*see* Fig. 55); renew if necessary.

If the cylinder head block to cylinder block joint is stiff because of the two faces having become gummed together, it is necessary to apply a few light taps to break the joint. Use a wooden mallet or a rawhide mallet applied at suitable points, and be most careful not to damage any of the horizontal fins during the tapping.

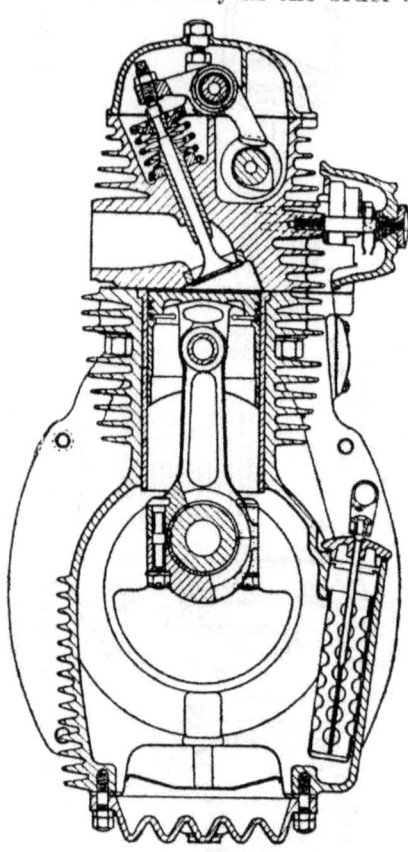

FIG. 56. SECTION THROUGH ENGINE SHOWING VALVE DISPOSITION, ETC.
(*From "Motor Cycle," London*)

After removing the cylinder head block, place it face downwards on a clean bench or on a table. It is important not to allow any hard foreign matter to come in pressure contact with the face of the head which is of a comparatively soft aluminium alloy and can readily be scratched or damaged. If occasion is had to remove any of the cylinder head studs, be particularly careful with the cylinder-head block face.

GENERAL MAINTENANCE AND OVERHAUL   87

To Remove the Overhead Rockers. To obtain access to the valves it is necessary first to remove the overhead rocker assembly. Referring to Fig. 29, unscrew the three nuts *C* holding the rocker shaft clip-lugs in place. Also remove the two nuts *D*. Then lift off the overhead rocker assembly bodily as illustrated in Fig. 57. Should the clip-lugs not slide freely over the studs, prise them off gently with a screwdriver or other suitable implement. Lay the complete overhead rocker assembly in a safe position, and then

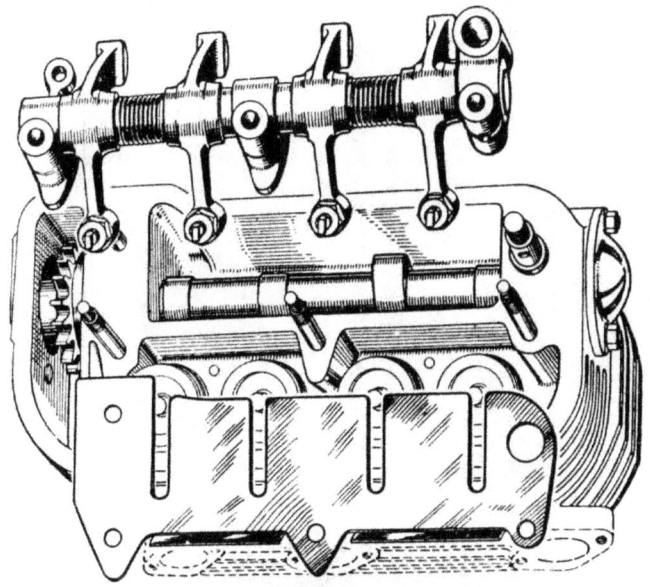

Fig. 57. Overhead Rocker Assembly Removed from Cylinder Head

proceed to remove the valves. Should the overhead rocker assembly be accidentally dismantled, *see* notes on page 96.

Removing the Valves. On the Sunbeam engine there are, of course, four valves, two inlet and two exhaust. Referring to Fig. 60, a hardened steel thimble is fitted to the end of each valve stem. This thimble is only a light press fit on the stem, and if it can readily be detached by hand, remove it to avoid the risk of accidental loss. Place all four thimbles in a safe position, and remember that during subsequent reassembly, the thimbles must on no account be omitted.

To remove each valve from its guide (*see* Fig. 58), use the Sunbeam valve spring compressor (*see* page 55) to press down on the valve spring top collar *A*, Fig. 59, until you can extract the two halves *B* of the split collet. If you find that the top collar (which has a tapered bore) binds on the split collet and prevents the halves being freed, apply a sharp tap to the edge of the collar as indicated in Fig. 60. The valve spring top collar, the duplex

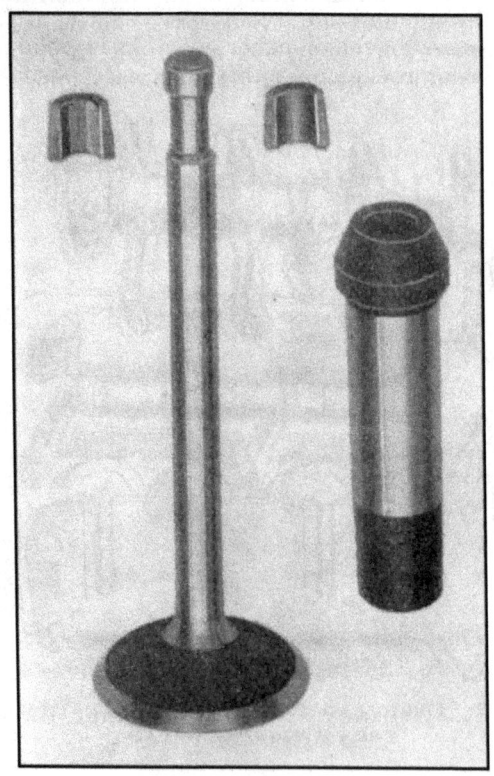

Fig. 58. Sunbeam Valve and its Guide
The split collets are shown inverted

valve spring, and the valve spring bottom collar can be removed as soon as the split collet is extracted, and the valve removed.

In a similar manner remove all four valve assemblies. Be very careful when you remove each valve to note its identity and location. The *valve* must be replaced in the guide from which it was withdrawn, because all of the valves are *individually ground* on to their seats and unless correctly replaced will not effect gas-tight seals. To avoid confusion it is also wise to identify for correct reassembly the valve spring collars, the valve springs, and the split collets.

GENERAL MAINTENANCE AND OVERHAUL

Removing Carbon Deposits. The formation and type of carbon deposits accumulating on the piston crowns and in the combustion chambers depend to a considerable degree upon whether or not the carburation is correct and how much wear of the cylinder bores and piston rings has occurred. Sometimes the deposits are soft and oily, but in other instances they may be very hard. Soft deposits can be removed very readily, but hard deposits are somewhat more difficult to eradicate, and great care must always be taken in scraping them off. Decarbonizing should always be thorough because carbon forms less quickly on smooth surfaces, and you do not want to decarbonize more often than is necessary!

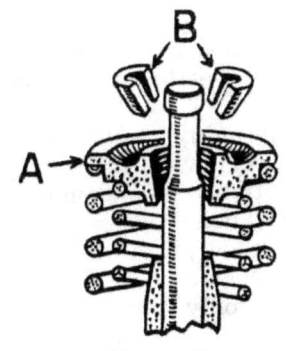

FIG. 59. VALVE SPRING REMOVAL

FIG. 60. TAPPING VALVE-SPRING TOP COLLAR TO FREE SPLIT-COLLET

Carefully scrape off all carbon deposits, using proprietary scrapers, or improvised tools such as slightly blunted screwdrivers or old wood chisels. Good proprietary scrapers designed for the job are undoubtedly best and can be obtained from most large accessory firms (see page 53). If the carbon deposits are very hard, the application of a little paraffin will help to soften the carbon and facilitate its removal.

Avoid scratching the soft aluminium alloy surfaces of the pistons and combustion chambers, and on no account attempt to use any abrasive such as emery cloth. Should any abrasive particles get between the piston rings and cylinder bores, the latter may become badly scored and possibly ruined. A new set of cylinder block liners is an expensive item. A point particularly worth noting is that scrapers should be reasonably sharp. It is possible to inflict far more harm on soft metal surfaces by using blunt scrapers somewhat impatiently than by using sharp ones with skill and discretion. Do not forget to remove all carbon deposits from the heads of the four valves, the vicinity of the valve ports, and the sparking plug holes. But be most careful not to scratch the seatings for the valves when the latter have been removed. After completing decarbonizing, scrupulously clean all surfaces with a slightly oily rag and leave no loose particles of carbon anywhere.

Grinding-in the Valves. As has been mentioned on page 82, it is desirable to inspect the valve faces and the cylinder head seatings each time the engine is decarbonized, but to grind-in the valves only if close inspection shows this to be *necessary*. The seatings in the cylinder head block deteriorate much more slowly than do the valve faces, and it is in most cases because of pitting of the valve faces that the valves have to be ground-in. Because they are subjected to higher temperatures, the exhaust valves require more attention than the inlet valves to restore them to their original smooth condition.

After cleaning the valve heads thoroughly, polish the valve stems (if they are discoloured and dirty) with some very fine emery cloth, using an up-and-down motion with the emery cloth held between the thumb and forefinger. Then if necessary grind-in each valve as described below, using a good proprietary grinding paste such as Richford's (obtainable in coarse and fine grades).

If the valve faces and seatings are only very slightly discoloured, a small amount of grinding-in with *fine* grade paste will quickly restore the valves to full efficiency. If, however, the exhaust valves have become widely, and perhaps deeply, pitted, a considerable amount of grinding-in, first with a coarse grade and then with a fine grade grinding paste, will probably be required.

Severe pitting caused through careless running with no valve clearances, a poor mixture, or late ignition timing, may necessitate radical treatment to restore valve efficiency, and it may be necessary to have the valve faces re-cut by the repair department of Sunbeam Motor Cycles, Ltd. (Montgomery Road, Birmingham 11). If the cylinder head valve seatings are also badly pitted, it is desirable to return the cylinder head block to the makers to have the seatings refaced. Bear in mind that any attempt to grind-in the valves excessively will cause the valves to become "pocketed," and this will adversely affect engine efficiency.

To grind-in a valve, smear a small quantity of suitable grinding paste on its bevelled edge, and replace the valve in its guide. Before replacing the valve it is a good plan to insert a light spring under the valve head to facilitate lifting the valve and rotating it to new positions during the grinding-in operation. Hold the valve stem with the special tool shown at 10 in Fig. 27 and oscillate the valve about a *quarter of a turn* backwards and

GENERAL MAINTENANCE AND OVERHAUL 91

forwards. When doing this, maintain a slight pull on the metal holder. Lift the valve every few oscillations and turn it to a new position.

Continue to grind-in a valve until a *continuous matt ring* (depth not important) is present on both the valve face and the seating in the cylinder head block. One application of grinding paste may be sufficient for an inlet valve, but several are usually required for exhaust valves. If a valve starts to "sing" during grinding-in, this shows that further grinding paste is needed.

After Grinding-in the Valves. Be careful to remove *all* traces of grinding paste. Thoroughly clean the valve faces, valve stems, and seatings with petrol or paraffin and a clean rag. To make sure that no abrasive has been left in the valve guides, it is a good plan to draw a clean rag through all four valve guides.

Valve Spring Renewal. After a considerable mileage has been covered it is desirable to renew the valve springs because heat and other factors reduce their efficiency. The exhaust valve springs are likely to require renewal before the inlet valve springs, being more heavily loaded and operating under considerably higher temperatures. Prior to reassembling the springs it is advisable to make a comparison check of their free lengths. To avoid the possible necessity of stripping-down parts specially in order to renew a spring or springs, when decarbonizing renew any spring whose free length is less than that of the other springs. It is, of course, highly unlikely that all four valve springs would weaken simultaneously.

Reassembling the Valves and Overhead Rockers. Replace each of the four valves in the following manner. Smear a little engine oil on the valve stem and replace the correct valve in the correct guide. Then fit the valve spring bottom collar, the duplex valve spring, and the valve spring top collar. With the Sunbeam valve spring compressor press down on the valve spring top collar A, Fig. 59, until you can replace the halves B of the split collet. If any difficulty is experienced in getting the split collet to "stay put" when releasing the pressure on the top collar, apply a little grease to the collet location on the valve stem. When each valve is replaced, be sure to fit the hardened steel thimble on the end of the valve stem. This must never be omitted. Tap the thimble right home.

Referring to Fig. 57, if the cam chamber baffle plate was previously removed, see that this is replaced, because it can rather easily be overlooked. Now position correctly and replace the overhead rocker assembly. Rotate the overhead rocker shaft so that its notches engage the three long mounting studs projecting vertically from the cylinder head block. Referring to Fig. 29, replace and tighten the three nuts C on the studs so as to lock the clip-lugs on the overhead rocker shaft. Also replace and tighten the two nuts (one of which is shown at D) on the front and rear clip-lugs. On the 1946-9 Model S7 engine there is only the front nut to be fitted. The extra lug is provided only on Models S8 and S7 de luxe.

To Replace the Cylinder Head Block. First make quite sure that the joint faces of the cylinder head block and the cylinder block are absolutely clean. Verify that the copper-asbestos gasket used for the joint is perfect, and replace this on the cylinder block face. Now carefully lower the cylinder head block into position.

With the appropriate spanners in the tool kit tighten down evenly and progressively the nuts, bolts, and studs securing the cylinder head block to the cylinder block. To prevent any risk of damaging or distorting the aluminium casting it is absolutely essential to tighten the eleven nuts, bolts, and studs in the correct sequence which is illustrated diagrammatically in Fig. 61. All should be tightened lightly first, and then about two to three further tightenings effected to obtain firm tightening, using always the correct sequence during each tightening. No final tightening of a nut, stud, or bolt should be attempted until all the others have already been tightened to the same degree. A cracked or distorted cylinder head would indeed be a serious misfortune. It should be noted here that a thoroughly gas-tight joint is essential to prevent "blowing" or loss of compression. The nuts, bolts, and studs previously referred to should therefore be tightened really firmly. The bolts and studs are made of a good steel which will withstand high stressing, and do not be afraid of damaging them.

Important Note. Referring to Fig. 61, Nos. 1 to 8 inclusive are the main holding-down bolts and must always be kept very firmly tightened. Nos. 9, 10, 11 are responsible only for sealing the rear joint face, and clearly very firm tightening of these is not of such paramount importance. After covering a short distance on the road, check Nos. 1-11 for tightness. This is *very* important.

Retiming the Valves. In order to remove the cylinder head block, the camshaft sprocket (E, Fig. 54) was previously removed. This, of course, necessitates retiming the valves after the cylinder head block and overhead valves have been replaced as already described on pages 91-92. Prior to the removal of the cylinder head block the engine (*see* page 84) was turned until the pistons were at top dead centre. For retiming the valves the pistons must remain at T.D.C. and if the engine has not been turned since the cylinder head block was removed, the piston position is correct for retiming. If the engine has been turned, further rotate it until the pistons are at true T.D.C. On the four-stroke Sunbeam engine the pistons reach T.D.C. once every engine revolution, and at true T.D.C. very slight backward or forward

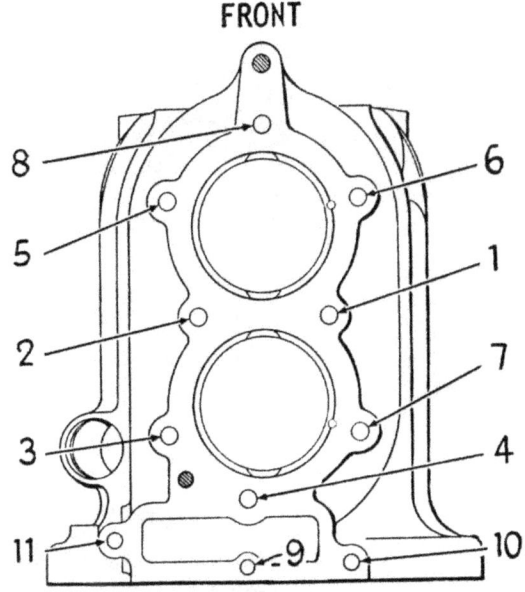

FIG. 61. DIAGRAM SHOWING CORRECT SEQUENCE FOR TIGHTENING NUTS, BOLTS, AND STUDS SECURING CYLINDER HEAD BLOCK

The same sequence should be used when removing the head

movement of the crankshaft does not cause the pistons to move up or down.

Retiming the valves should present no difficulty. Referring to Fig. 54, rotate the overhead camshaft slowly until the driving peg hole *A* in the end face of the rear journal is aligned vertically above the camshaft as shown. Hold the camshaft sprocket *E* and engage it with the camshaft driving chain such that its driving peg is in true alignment with the driving peg hole *A*. Now slide the sprocket (*without moving the chain relatively to the teeth*) into position so that the sprocket driving peg enters hole *A*. The replacement of the camshaft driving chain and the camshaft sprocket is considerably facilitated if the automatic chain tensioner is first unscrewed (*see* page 65). Note that on the earlier type S7 engine (up to September, 1948) the camshaft chain tensioner has no adjustment as shown in Fig. 35 and it is necessary to remove the inspection cover or screwed plug (1949–57), and then pull back the spring-loaded tensioner blade as illustrated in Fig. 62. Finally replace bolt *D* (Fig. 54); tighten securely. The valve timing must be correct if the foregoing instructions are followed exactly.

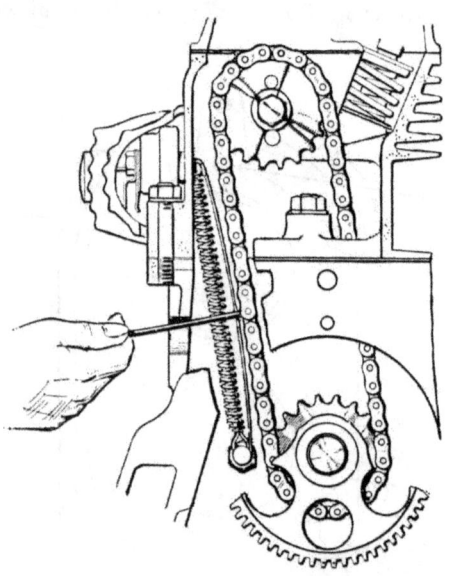

Fig. 62. Pulling Back Automatic Chain Tensioner when Fitting Camshaft Driving Chain and Sprocket
Applicable to earlier S7 engines. *See also* Fig. 35

For the benefit of those who at some time or other for some reason may wish to check the valve timing, using a degree disk attached to the crankshaft, it may be mentioned that for all Sunbeam engines the timing is as tabulated below.

Valve Timing on 1946 and Subsequent Engines

Model	Inlet Opens	Inlet Closes	Exhaust Opens	Exhaust Closes
S7 S7 de luxe S8	45° before T.D.C.	70° after B.D.C.	65° before B.D.C.	35° after T.D.C.

GENERAL MAINTENANCE AND OVERHAUL 95

Retiming the Ignition. Like the retiming of the valves, this is perfectly straightforward, and the timing is bound to be correct if the distributor unit is correctly replaced, which should be done in the following manner. When you have positioned the camshaft driving sprocket exactly as described in the preceding paragraph (Retiming the Valves) you will observe that the peg hole in the sprocket immediately below the centre of the driving sprocket is unoccupied. This second peg hole receives the driven peg of the distributor coupling flange. Rotate the coupling flange until the driven peg is aligned with the unoccupied hole in the camshaft driving sprocket (i.e. vertically below its centre), when the centres of the slots in the external fixing flange are in line with the distributor securing studs.

Now carefully position the distributor unit the right way up (low tension leads below) in the cylinder-head block housing so that the peg in the distributor coupling flange enters the hole in the camshaft sprocket. Afterwards tighten lightly the two nuts on the distributor securing studs.

Note that the coupling flange of the distributor body is pinned permanently to the spindle. Thus if you engage the driving peg as already described, the ignition timing is automatically correct within the range of adjustment provided by the slots on the flange of the distributor body. Marks are to be found on the slots and it is best to set the distributor unit in accordance with these marks. When this has been done it only remains to tighten on the studs the two distributor-retaining nuts.

To Check the Ignition Timing. After replacing the distributor unit in accordance with the instructions just given, the ignition timing is sure to be correct. But if, for curiosity or for some other reason, you desire to check the accuracy of the ignition timing, you can do this as described below.

Rotate the engine so that the pistons are at T.D.C., with the *front* piston in the firing position. In this position both valves should, of course, be closed, and you can verify this point by feeling the overhead rockers and noting that there is a clearance between the rockers and valve stem thimbles. Now observe the distributor rocker arm and the contact-breaker. If the ignition timing is correct, the rotor arm should point to the *off-side* and the contacts should be commencing to open. To ascertain whether in fact the contacts are just opening, you can turn the engine slowly to and fro and watch the action of the contacts.

Before Replacing the Cylinder Head Cover. Check and if necessary adjust the valve clearances in accordance with the instructions given on page 58. If you have ground-in the valves, it is possible that the clearances have become appreciably reduced.

Final Reassembly. After checking the valve clearances, replace the cylinder head cover, the cover for the camshaft chain tunnel (located below the distributor unit), the carburettor, and the exhaust pipes and silencer. Make certain that the gasket for the carburettor flange and the two gaskets for the exhaust pipe flanges are perfect. If they are not, renew them.

Replace both sparking plugs and their high tension leads. Also re-connect the oil pressure indicator lead and then fit the cover for the sparking plugs. Finally connect up the fuel pipe, turn on the petrol, and run up the engine to check that everything is satisfactory. After covering approximately 20 miles check for tightness the nuts, bolts, and studs securing the cylinder head (*see* page 92). If any are not firmly tightened, apply the appropriate spanners as required.

MAJOR OVERHAUL

When a very big mileage has been covered and the engine begins to show indications of wear and tear, accompanied by some noise and a decline in performance, it is advisable to subject the machine to a major overhaul which entails removing the engine and gearbox unit from the frame, stripping-down the engine and machine, and effecting such adjustments and renewals as are called for.

A major overhaul cannot be undertaken by the average motorcyclist, as generally he has neither the sufficient technical skill nor the facilities required. The designers of the Sunbeam have paid special attention to accessibility and ease of maintenance, but complete stripping-down and overhaul need considerable skill. Unless you have sound mechanical skill and knowledge, and also a workshop bench, you are not advised to embark on an ambitious programme of stripping-down and reconditioning, but to entrust this work to the makers or a firm specializing in Sunbeam service and overhaul.

Dismantling the Overhead Rocker Assembly. Only in special circumstances (e.g. suspected wear of the overhead rocker bushes) is it necessary to dismantle the overhead rocker assembly. This should be done after dismantling the engine as described on pages 82–87. Occasionally the rocker assembly is accidentally dismantled after being removed from the supporting studs on the cylinder head block, the spacing springs (*see* Fig. 63) forcing the rockers apart. It is important to note the positions of the various components to ensure correct reassembly, and they are clearly shown in Fig. 63. Observe particularly that the overhead rocker shaft is *notched* for correct location in the cylinder head block studs. Before attempting to replace the overhead rocker assembly in the cylinder head block it is absolutely essential to turn the rocker mounting shaft to the position shown in Fig. 63.

To Remove the Overhead Camshaft. The overhead camshaft can readily be removed for inspection of the cams and camshaft bearings after removing the overhead rocker assembly (*see* pages 87–88), but removal of the camshaft is seldom called for. To

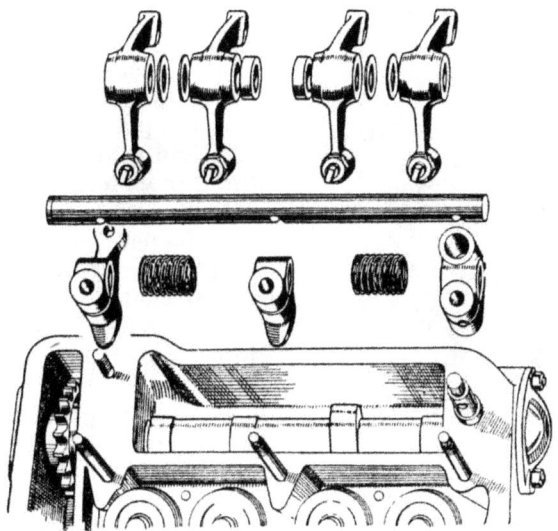

Fig. 63. Exploded View of Overhead Rocker Assembly

remove the camshaft, first lift off the baffle plate (*see* Fig. 57) which covers the cam chamber.

Referring to Fig. 64, now remove the two securing nuts and take off the cap *A* from the end of the camshaft housing (at the front of the cylinder head block). Removal of the cap exposes the hexagon head *B* of the bolt which secures the camshaft and locating thrust washer *C*. Unscrew this bolt and draw the camshaft out from the rear through the hole which comprises the mounting for the distributor unit. When removing the hexagon-headed bolt just referred to, insert a piece of soft metal *D* between a cam flank and the side of the cam chamber. To reassemble the camshaft, reverse the above dismantling procedure.

To Remove the Engine and Gearbox Unit from the Frame. Before this can be done it is necessary to remove the exhaust system, the carburettor, the distributor, and the dynamo. An exploded view of the dynamo is shown in Fig. 65 and the attachment of the end plate and yoke to the crankcase, and the armature to the end of the crankshaft, are clearly shown. It is important to note that the central securing bolt has a *left-hand thread*.

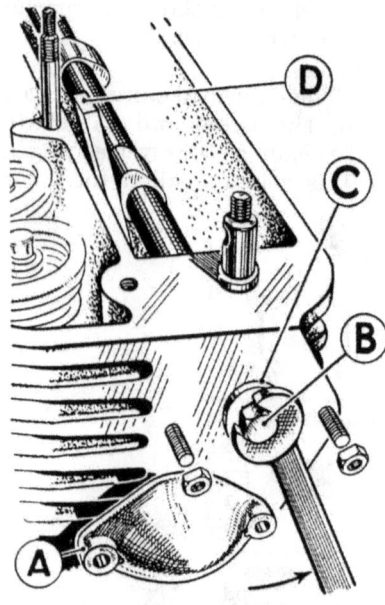

Fig. 64. Removing the Overhead Camshaft

Remove the engine sump drain plug and the gearbox filling cap and drain the engine and gearbox thoroughly. Complete draining is most readily effected after a run when the oil is warm. Afterwards, to prevent accidental loss, replace the plug and cap and tighten them lightly. Be careful not to forget the fibre washers.

Disconnect the fuel pipe and drain the tank prior to removing it. Note that two rubber cushions are provided to insulate the tank from the frame top tube. Next disconnect the speedometer drive on top of the gearbox, and take off the Lucas battery, control box, and the battery container. You need not disconnect the lighting harness as the leads are sufficiently long to enable the boxes to be laid on top of the

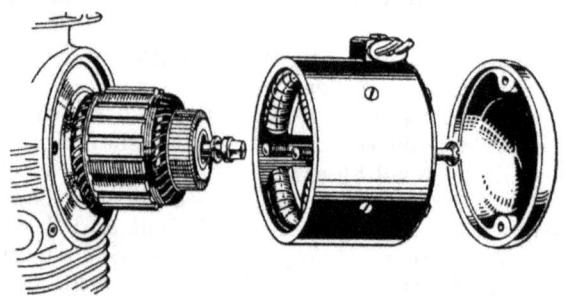

Fig. 65. Exploded View of Dynamo

saddle. It is necessary, however, to unclip the distributor cover. Disconnect the engine steady stay where fitted.

Disconnect the clutch operating cable at the gearbox end, and the two bolts *A* (Fig. 66) on the universal joint at the front end

GENERAL MAINTENANCE AND OVERHAUL

of the drive shaft. Observe in connexion with subsequent assembly that the bushes for the universal joint bolts are spigoted in pairs on alternate sides. Note also that the forks at each end of the drive shaft must be in proper alignment.

Referring to Fig. 67, it is also necessary (on Models S8 and S7 de luxe) to remove the engine damper plate D. First remove the nut shown at M. This releases the spring pressure unit on the damper plate. Next withdraw the two attachment bolts E by unscrewing their securing nuts. The damper plate can now be removed, together with its four reinforced plates C and the friction disk F. Remove the lower frame clip nut and its bolt B to release the tongue A, and loosen (not remove) the upper frame clip nut and slide the frame clip bracket O along the frame top tube to a convenient position.

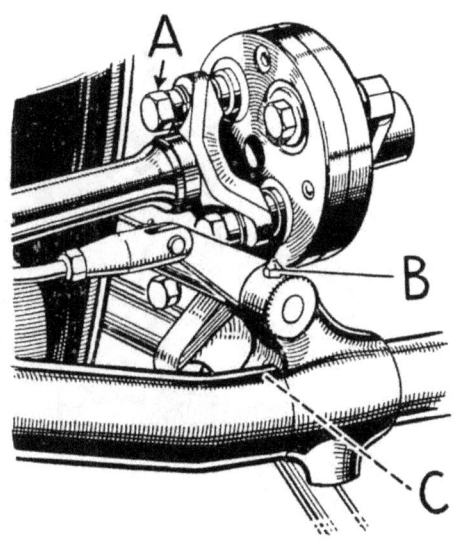

Fig. 66. Front Universal Joint

Having removed the various items as already described, you can start actually to remove the engine and gearbox unit from the frame. Two rubber cushions (shown at A and B in Fig. 36) are provided to ensure a flexible mounting for the power unit. One cushion is at the rear of the gearbox, and the other one at a point level with the cylinder head joint face above the Lucas dynamo. Before attempting to remove these cushions, take the weight off the power unit by placing a wooden block of suitable thickness beneath the engine sump. Now remove the various nuts and bolts securing the power unit to the frame, but do not remove the frame front cross member. Finally raise the power unit clear of the frame and lift away from the *off-side*.

To Replace the Engine and Gearbox Unit in the Frame. The installation of the power unit in the frame can be effected by reversing the procedure used for removal and already described. However, the undermentioned points should be carefully noted.

Referring to Fig. 67, after replacing the power unit in the frame and bolting up the main pair of pre-set rubber mountings (shown at A and B in Fig. 36), fit the tongue A to the frame clip bracket.

Tighten the nut on the lower retaining bolt *B*, but at this stage do not tighten the upper bolt. Next refit loosely the four reinforcing plates on either side of the damper plate *D* with the two nuts and bolts *E*. Make sure that the bevelled edges are away from the damper plate as indicated in Fig. 67. Position the friction disk *F* and move the damper plate, together with the frame clip

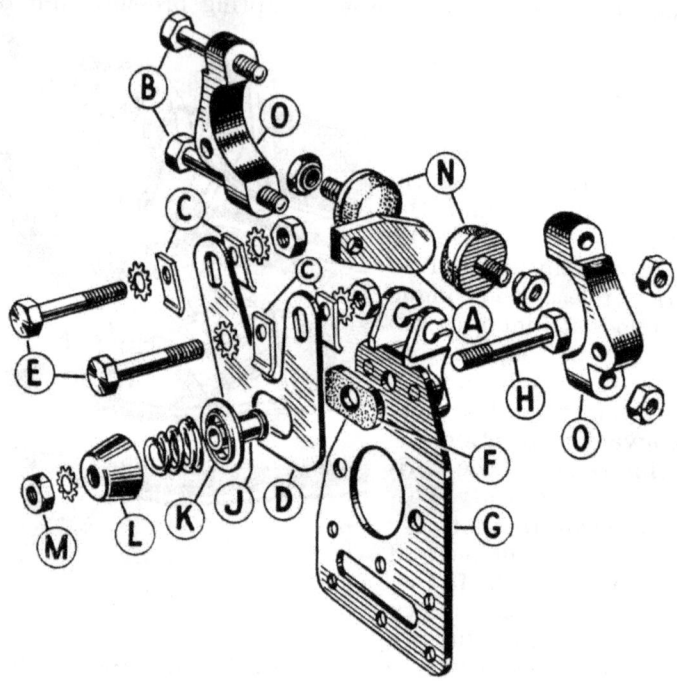

Fig. 67. Engine Damper Plate, Snubber Plate, Snubbers, and Associated Fittings at the Top Rear of Engine (1949 onwards)

The position of the snubber plate *G* on the engine is indicated at *C* in Fig. 36

bracket, forwards until the friction disk is gripped lightly between the snubber plate *G* and the damper plate.

Fit the bolt *H* and the distance piece *J*, and position the damper plate *D* so that the distance piece is centrally located in the damper plate hole. The damper plate holes, by the way, are elongated to permit of the engine damper snubbers being adjusted. Replace the washer and spring *K*, the cap *L*, and the nut *M*. Tighten the nut so that the cap is locked against the distance piece *J*.

GENERAL MAINTENANCE AND OVERHAUL

Adjusting the Engine Damper Snubbers. After installing the power unit in the frame, you must adjust the damper fittings correctly. Detailed instructions for doing this are given on page 66.

Removing the Big-end Bearings. The big-end bearings (see Fig. 68) can be dismantled with the power unit installed in the frame, but for obvious reasons their dismantling is much more readily effected after the power unit has been taken out of the frame as previously described. Where it is desired to remove the connecting rods and pistons, it is always advisable to take the power unit right out.

Prior to dismantling the big-end bearings, first withdraw the engine sump and filter tray after removing the twelve securing nuts from the crankcase studs. Be careful with the joint washers. If damaged during removal, they must be renewed. The big-end bearings are exposed as soon as the filter tray is removed. Turn the engine crankshaft until the big-ends are at bottom dead centre. Then remove the split-pins and nuts from the two bolts which secure each bearing cap to its connecting rod. Make a mental note of the tightness of the nuts so that you can tighten them to the same extent during subsequent reassembly.

Big-end Bearing Renewal. White-metal Vandervell liners comprise the big-end bearings, and these are obtainable ready for immediate fitting to the connecting rods. Actually renewal is called for only at very long intervals and it is quite unnecessary to undertake any scraping or fitting (used in the proper sense of the word). If you remove the big-end bearing caps in order to renew the bearing liners, remember that the caps must be replaced in their original positions. In the case of each connecting rod, one of the bearing cap bolt bosses is marked (on the near-side of the engine), and this mark must correspond with a similar mark on the bearing cap.

If the crankpin journals have worn oval more than a few thousandths of an inch after a very big mileage, it will probably be necessary to have them re-ground, and big-end liners of undersize internal diameter (obtainable from the Sunbeam service department or from local dealers) will be required. The fitting of undersize liners is, of course, rarely called for.

To Remove the Pistons and Connecting Rods. When you have removed the big-end bearing caps as previously described it is possible to withdraw the pistons and connecting rods from the tops of the cylinder bores (see Fig. 69). Note that special care is required when doing this, because the overall width of the connecting-rod big-ends is only slightly less than that of the cylinder

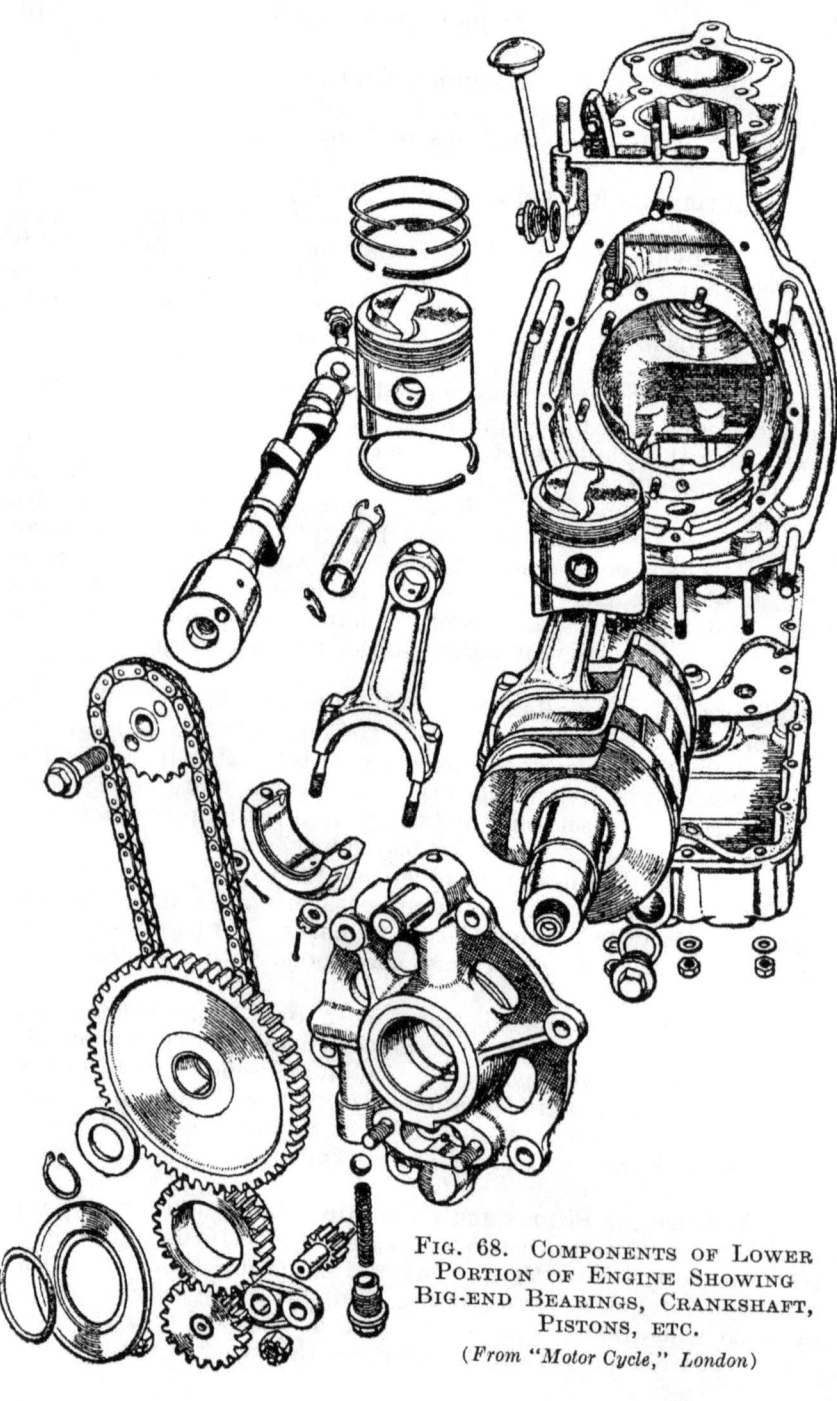

FIG. 68. COMPONENTS OF LOWER PORTION OF ENGINE SHOWING BIG-END BEARINGS, CRANKSHAFT, PISTONS, ETC.

(*From "Motor Cycle," London*)

bores. Indeed, the heads of the big-end bolts are machined to provide just sufficient clearances. Before attempting to slide the connecting rods into the cylinder bores it is important to turn the

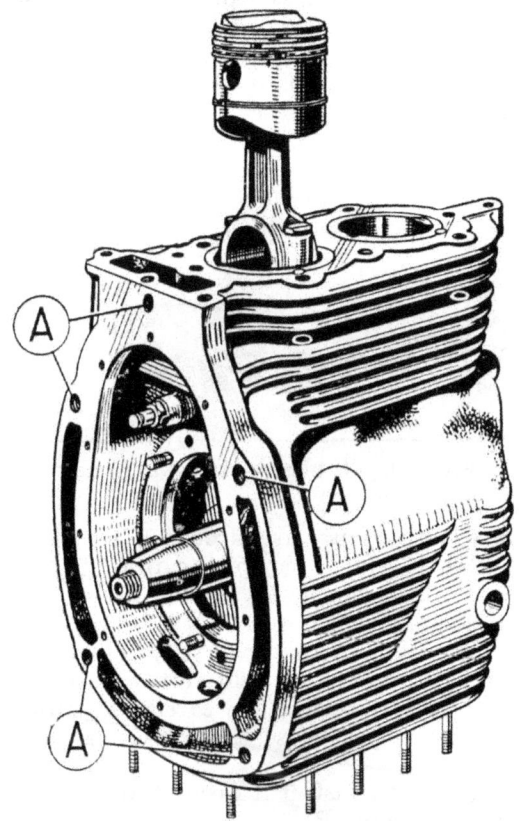

FIG. 69. SHOWING HOW PISTONS AND CONNECTING RODS ARE WITHDRAWN FROM THE TOP OF THE ONE-PIECE CYLINDER BLOCK AND CRANKCASE

At *A* are five holes for the studs securing the gearbox unit

big-end bolts to the correct positions. Unless you do this, you incur some risk of scoring the cylinder bores badly.

To Remove the Pistons from the Connecting Rods. Generally the primary object in removing the pistons is to examine the rings and skirts for condition and wear. Heavy oil consumption, piston slap, and reduced engine performance are caused by worn rings, pistons, and cylinder bores. Look for signs of blackening and scorching on the upper parts of the piston skirts. Also check the piston diameters at various points with a micrometer to see whether they are in accordance with the maker's maximum wear figures.

The gudgeon-pins securing the pistons to the connecting rods are of the fully-floating type and, as may be seen in Fig. 70, each pin is located in the piston bosses by two circlips. Remove these with a small pair of snipe-nosed pliers. After the circlips have been removed it is advisable to scrap them in case they have been over-stressed or damaged. A faulty circlip can cause most serious damage if it comes adrift with the engine running.

With the engine cold, the gudgeon-pin is often rather a tight fit in the bosses of the piston, though it is a free running fit when

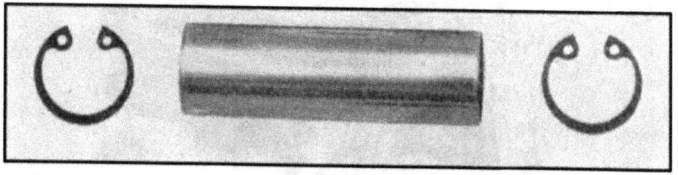

FIG. 70. GUDGEON-PIN AND CIRCLIPS

the engine has warmed up to its normal running temperature. It is a good plan to warm the piston prior to tapping out the gudgeon-pin, by wrapping a rag soaked in hot water around it for a few minutes. Actual removal of the pin should be effected by using a gudgeon-pin extractor of proprietary make, or else by driving it out with a hammer and soft-nose drift or punch. If you employ the latter method, be careful to support the piston on the opposite side, otherwise there is a risk of distorting the piston.

After removing each piston it is advisable to scratch an "F" on the inside to indicate which is the front and so ensure correct replacement which is absolutely essential. The standard compression ratio is 6·5 to 1, but on export models the compression ratio is generally 6·8 to 1 or 7·2 to 1. Pistons giving the higher compression ratios are not reversible, even when new, as they have specially shaped heads; wrong replacement is almost impossible. Be careful not to mix up the pistons. Each must be replaced the correct way round in the cylinder liner bore from which it was removed. Fig. 71 shows the standard piston.

Removing the Piston Rings. Do not disturb the rings more often than is necessary: if compression remains good, leave them alone. The rings are made of cast-iron and, being very brittle, they cannot safely be sprung out wider than the width of the piston crowns. The safest method of removing the rings is to insert beneath each ring at equal distances three strips of thin gauge sheet metal about ¼ in. wide. When removing the three upper rings, remove the scraper ring first and work upwards.

FIG. 71. STANDARD PISTON GIVING 6·5 TO 1 COMPRESSION RATIO

Note the two drilled grooves for the scraper rings. Prior to 1949 the lower scraper ring groove was omitted

To remove rings stuck with carbon, apply some paraffin, and as a last resort use a proprietary ring removal tool.

Inspecting the Piston Rings. The piston rings (*see* Fig. 72) are the mainguard of engine compression and upon them largely depends the efficient conversion of heat inside the combustion chambers to powerful downward piston thrusts. They must have a polished surface all round, be free but not slack in their grooves, have good springiness, and have their gaps equally spaced and of the correct size. Inspect the rings closely for general condition. If inspection shows that the surfaces are bright all round, the rings are obviously making good circumferential contact with the cylinder liner bores and can be regarded as serviceable. Renew any rings which are found to be discoloured or scored. Also renew any which have lost their original springiness, are vertically loose in their grooves, or have gaps which are outside the permissible limits specified by Sunbeam Motor Cycles, Ltd. Clean the rings thoroughly on their inside faces and the ends of the rings, also the slots in the scraper rings (*see* Fig. 72). New compression and scraper rings are 0·064 in. and 0·0156 in. wide respectively.

The most satisfactory method of inspecting the piston rings for wear is to insert them squarely in the cylinder bores after the

FIG. 72. THE SUNBEAM PISTON RINGS

Each piston has two compression rings (*left*) and two slotted scraper rings (*right*). On pre-1949 pistons only one scraper ring is fitted

pistons have been removed and then check their gaps with suitable feeler gauges. The normal piston ring gap is 0·004 in.–0·006 in. (0·1 mm–0·15 mm), and the maximum permissible gap is 0·020 in. (0·50 mm). If the ring gaps are found to exceed considerably the above-mentioned dimensions, much wear has occurred and ring renewal is called for.

It is worth noting that the increase in gap over the original figure, divided by three, gives the approximate diametral wear. Some of this may be on the bore, and some on the rings. If you first check the bore wear, the wear on the rings can be accurately decided. The foregoing remarks apply to all four rings. An experienced mechanic can generally further assess wear by closely examining the bearing surfaces of the rings. Note that you can often cure a tendency for heavy oil consumption by renewing the scraper rings, provided that excessive cylinder liner bore wear has not occurred.

GENERAL MAINTENANCE AND OVERHAUL

Cylinder Liner Bore Wear. After a very big mileage reconditioning of the cylinder liner bores may be required. The liner bores can be re-ground up to 0·010 in. oversize, or if the wear exceeds this figure, new Brivadium (2¾ in. or 70 mm bore) can be fitted. Re-boring, of course, necessitates the fitting of oversize pistons. The cylinder block liners are detachable and can be tapped out with a suitable mallet and punch from below. The front and rear liners are different and are not interchangeable. See that the liners pick up on the locating dowels in the cylinder block.

Dismantling the Timing Gear. The timing gear is of simple design and very accessible as may be seen in Fig. 54. To dismantle the timing gear it is first necessary to remove the clutch flywheel (*see* page 112). A thin gauge sheet metal partition is then exposed. This partition carries a spring-loaded oil seal for the main shaft and is secured to the crankcase face by ten cheese-headed screws which can be wired or provided with vibration-proof washers. Remove the ten screws and withdraw the partition plate. Also remove the fabric washer behind the partition plate and be careful not to damage the former. Now remove the flange washer from the main shaft, and remember that this washer must be fitted on reassembly.

The top screw is considerably longer than the others and it prevents the timing chain from becoming jammed in the timing chest or accidentally falling down. Referring to Fig. 54, when removing the cam sprocket E, always replace the top screw *before* you remove the bolt D. This precaution may save much bother. Remove the circlip H from the spindle J and also the washer behind it. Disengage the chain from the sprocket E by easing it off the sprocket teeth, and then slide the half-time pinion off the spindle. Finally detach the camshaft chain and its automatic spring-loaded tensioner. The tensioner is located on the pin M.

Concerning the Oil Pump. The pump is built into the rear bearing housing shown at P in Fig. 54. A dismantled pump is shown in Fig. 73. Two studs and nuts secure the cover plate to the housing. For locking purposes the nuts are slotted and wired. Do not remove the driving pinion R unless this is genuinely necessary. The driving pinion is a press fit on its spindle, and is secured by a tapered pin.

To Remove the Crankshaft. After removing the gearbox (*see* page 109), dismantling the timing gears, and possibly dismantling the oil pump unit, as previously described, draw off the engine shaft pinion shown at S in Fig. 54. It is necessary to use an extractor as the pinion is a tight fit on the crankshaft. Remove the key from the crankshaft key-way and put it in a safe place pending reassembly.

Remove the dynamo from the front end of the crankshaft (*see* page 98) if you have not already done this. Also remove the two connecting rods from the crankshaft journals (*see* page 101) if these have not yet been removed.

Now remove the rear bearing housing shown at *P* in Fig. 54 by removing the six securing nuts and sliding the housing off the

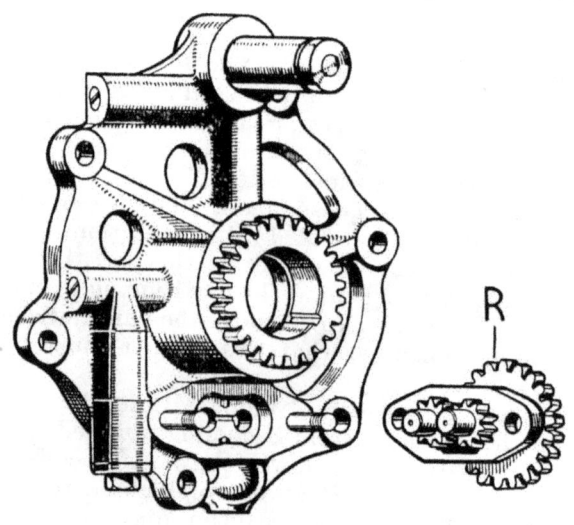

Fig. 73. Oil Pump Unit Shown Dismantled

studs. The crankshaft (*see* Fig. 69) can now be withdrawn from the crankcase by pulling it to the rear. Should the front of the crankshaft be tight in the front bearing, release it by applying a few taps with a mallet or soft punch. After withdrawing the crankshaft you can if you wish press or drive out the front bearing itself. A circlip fitted to a groove in the front bearing housing locates the bearing in one direction. At the front of the circlip there is a spring-loaded oil seal. Be careful with this. Note that if the rear main journal of the crankshaft has worn oval more than a few thousandths of an inch, you will have to have it re-ground and a main bearing of undersize internal diameter fitted. A suitable bearing is obtainable from a local Sunbeam dealer or from the service department of Sunbeam Motor Cycles, Ltd.

Reassembling the Engine. To reassemble the engine after crankshaft renewal is quite straightforward, but to ensure the

GENERAL MAINTENANCE AND OVERHAUL

valve timing being correct there are a few points to watch. Referring to Fig. 54, after replacing the rear bearing housing *P* and the engine shaft pinion *S*, turn the pinion and crankshaft until the key-ways (and key) are vertically upwards as indicated. Place the half-time gear *K* on its spindle so that the two teeth marked with two dots engage the tooth on the engine shaft pinion which is in vertical alignment with the key-ways and has the tooth marked with a single dot as shown in Fig. 54. The timing gears, etc., are now correctly assembled for the final valve timing operation, which should be effected as described on page 92.

If the oil pump cover plate has been previously removed, replace this before replacing the rear bearing housing. Use a new length of 19 S.W.G. soft copper or iron wire to lock the nuts. Tighten the nuts securing the rear bearing housing and do not omit to fit the spring washers. With the exception of the large circlips in the front bearing housing, renew all tab-washers, circlips, and split-pins.

Removing the Gearbox. With the power unit taken out of the frame, it is a simple matter to remove the gearbox and if necessary dismantle it. Dismantling should not be necessary except in order to renew a worn or damaged part. To remove the gearbox, unscrew the five nuts from the studs (their position is shown at *A* in Fig. 69) and withdraw the complete gearbox. When the gearbox is withdrawn the clutch assembly remains in position on the engine crankshaft, the front end of the gearbox mainshaft being splined to engage the clutch centre.

To Dismantle the Gearbox. With the gearbox removed from the engine as previously described, it is a simple matter to strip it down. Remove the pinch-bolts which engage grooves in the foot gear-change and kick-starter pedal shafts and withdraw the pedals from their shafts, which are splined to provide alternative pedal positions. Next remove the gearbox side cover plate (complete with kick-starter and foot gear-change mechanism) after undoing the eight large cheese-headed securing screws. Also remove the gear indicator.

Withdraw the universal joint coupling and its flange from the rear of the layshaft after removing the split-pin and the centrally located nut. Remove the clutch operating rod from the centre of the gearbox mainshaft. Withdraw it from the front end of the gearbox and also remove the circlip locating the mainshaft kick-starter ratchet on the splined rear end of the mainshaft.

Unlock the tab-washers and then remove the eight nuts securing the gearbox front bearing housing to the gearbox shaft inside the clutch bell. Now withdraw the front bearing housing. You can then remove the gearbox mainshaft, the layshaft, and the selector shaft, complete with the gear train which comes away in one assembly (*see* Fig. 74). If you wish to do so, you can now dismantle the gear train on the bench, but before doing this,

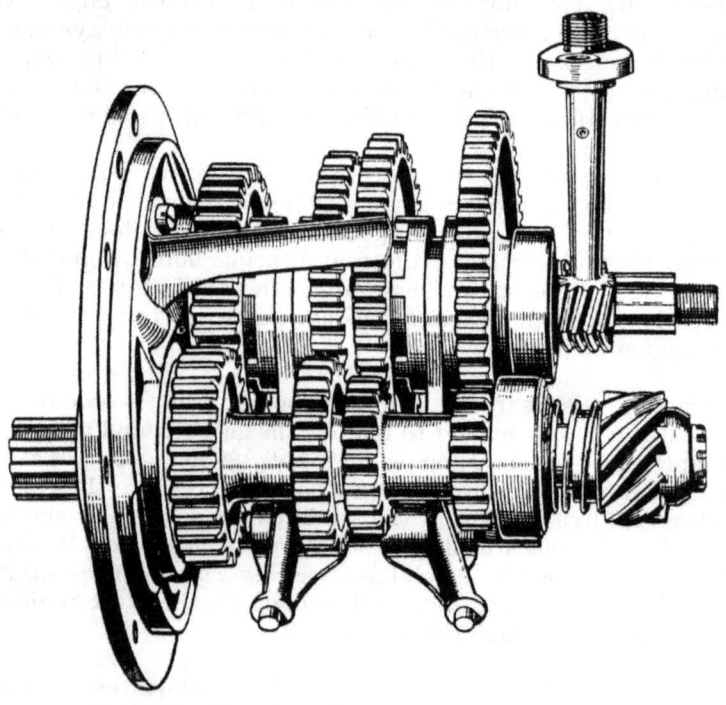

Fig. 74. Sunbeam Four-speed Gear Train

be very careful to note the relative positions of the various components, so as to ensure correct reassembly.

Dismantling the Foot Gear-change. As may be seen in Fig. 75, the main components are: (1) the shaft A with its operating arm B; (2) the cam actuating plate C; (3) the pawl plate D; and (4) the cam and ratchet plate E. Referring to Fig. 75, F is the cam actuating plate fulcrum; G the two pawls; H the ratchet teeth on the cam plate; J the cam grooves; K the peg on the ratchet plate for the rod L connected to lever M; N the indicator sleeve; P the pawl spring; and R the large hairpin spring.

If you decide for any reason to strip down the foot gear-change mechanism (not advised unless really necessary), see that the pawl spring P is correctly re-engaged on assembly with the pawls

GENERAL MAINTENANCE AND OVERHAUL

as shown in Fig. 75. Also make sure that the large hairpin spring *R* (a double-acting return spring for the pedal) engages correctly the operating arm *B*.

To Reassemble the Gearbox. Assemble the parts in the reverse order in which they were dismantled (*see* page 109). Depress the kick-starter once or twice to facilitate sliding the gearbox end

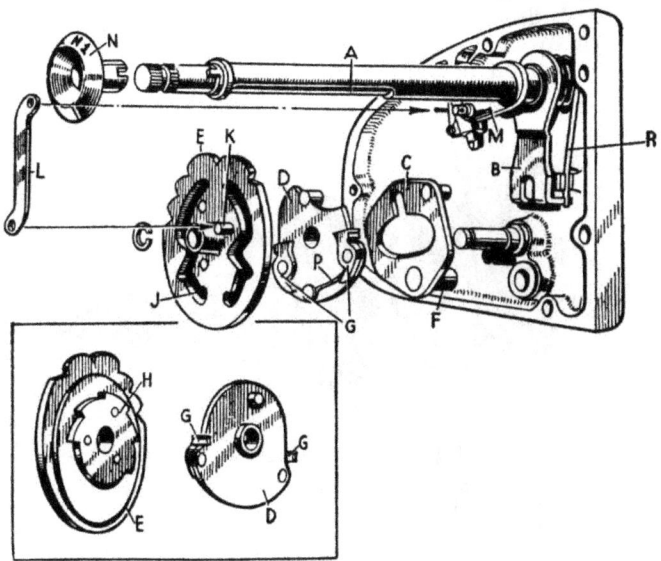

FIG. 75. DETAILS OF FOOT GEAR-CHANGE MECHANISM

cover home. On no account forget to replace the clutch operating rod in the hollow mainshaft.

Prior to replacing the gearbox end cover finally, it is important to check that the pegs on the ends of the gear selector sliding fork engage correctly in the cam grooves in the foot gear-change cam plate. Place the gears in neutral (between first and second gears), and turn the foot gear-change mechanism also to the neutral position as indicated by the engagement of the locating plunger (close to *M* in Fig. 75) in the appropriate notch on the edge of the cam plate. With the gears registering correctly, you should experience no difficulty in sliding the gearbox cover plate home readily.

The Speedometer Drive. You can detach this as a complete unit before or after dismantling the gearbox. The unit is bolted to the top of the gearbox. To remove it, disconnect the central union nut coupling the cable to the drive, lift this away, and then remove the two securing nuts. Now withdraw the speedometer drive, complete with the pinion.

To Remove the Clutch. As has been mentioned on page 109, the clutch remains in position on the engine crankshaft when the gearbox is removed. The clutch rarely requires attention, as it is of sturdy design and well able to withstand big power transmission with little wear. Eventually, however, and especially if the clutch has been permitted to slip unduly, the friction linings do become worn down. This necessitates dismantling the clutch

FIG. 76. THE CLUTCH SHOWN DISMANTLED

From March, 1948, the rubber in the centre of the driven plate was modified to steel as shown. Prior to March, 1949, the clutch flywheel was somewhat different

and renewing the fabric rings constituting the friction linings. The friction member is shown at C in Fig. 76.

The clutch, unlike the gear train inside the gearbox, cannot be removed as a complete unit, but the dismantling of the various components is perfectly simple. Remove the clutch spring adjuster nuts shown at A from the six driving pegs. Unscrew these nuts evenly, and exercise considerable care during their final removal which releases the clutch spring pressure.

Now withdraw in this order: the outer clutch plate B; the clutch centre or driven (friction) plate C; and the inner or spring pressure plate. Remove the six springs and put them safely on one side. Only the flywheel (which serves as the clutch body) now remains in position. To remove the flywheel, unlock the tab-washer securing the nut D on the mainshaft and remove the nut itself which has a right-hand thread and is always tightened very securely. You may be able to remove nut D by hand pressure only, in which case use a box spanner and long tommy-bar giving ample leverage, or a special tubular spanner, while preventing the flywheel from turning with a suitable lever. If

GENERAL MAINTENANCE AND OVERHAUL 113

you cannot shift the nut by hand pressure, use a hammer on the spanner. In this case you need not hold the flywheel with a lever because its own inertia suffices to prevent turning.

After removing the flywheel securing nut, withdraw the flywheel from the mainshaft. It is a tight fit on the taper shaft and it may be necessary to deliver a few sharp taps with a copper or rawhide mallet to the face of the flywheel rim. On no account must heavy blows be delivered, or there is a risk of distorting or damaging the flywheel. If the above procedure does not loosen the flywheel, an extractor tool of the "pulley drawer" type may be required to withdraw the flywheel. A suitable extractor is referred to on page 55. Unless you are thoroughly experienced, it is recommended that a proper extractor always be used for withdrawing the flywheel. After taking off the flywheel, remove the key from the mainshaft and put it in a safe place. For reassembly, a special clutch assembly tool is needed (*see* page 56).

Inspecting the Clutch After Dismantling. Examine the clutch driven member shown at C in Fig. 76. If the fabric linings are badly worn, relining is essential. Skilled motor-cyclists can undertake the relining themselves, but the clutch driven member can if preferred be forwarded to the Sunbeam repair department or submitted to a local dealer for relining.

Inspect the steel driving plates for deep scoring caused through excessive clutch slip. Such scoring should be removed by smoothing off and rubbing down on a surface plate. If the scoring is so bad that the plates cannot be satisfactorily reconditioned, there is no alternative but to renew the plates concerned.

Check the free length of the clutch springs. This in the case of new springs is 1·55 in., and if the free length of the springs which have been removed is much less than the figure just quoted, the springs have obviously collapsed under the influence of excessive heat, and immediate renewal is called for.

To Dismantle the Rear Drive. It is assumed that the rear wheel has been removed as described on page 71. Also disconnect the rear brake lever by removing the nut from the cam spindle (shown at A in Fig. 78). Next remove the two bolts A (Fig. 66) and disconnect the front universal joint. Note that if this universal joint (or the rear one) is detached completely, you must reassemble it with the spigoted sleeves positioned as shown in Fig. 66.

Unscrew the filler cap and drain plug shown at D and E respectively in Fig. 15, and drain the oil off, preferably when warm after a run. Remove the seven nuts from the studs securing the worm gear casing to the frame (and to the rear cover plate which is also part of the off-side plunger of the rear suspension). Then take off the complete worm drive and lay it on a clean bench ready for further dismantling. It is best, however, to remove the complete unit from the frame and then dismantle it.

Referring to Fig. 77, in order to remove the worm, first remove

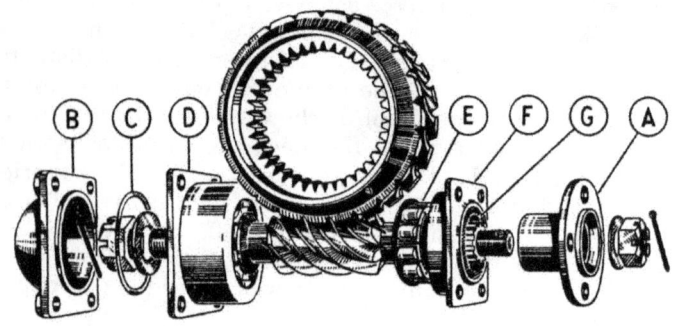

FIG. 77. COMPONENTS OF THE REAR DRIVE

the split-pin and the nut from the front end of the housing and then withdraw the coupling flange *A* splined to the worm shaft. Now remove the four nuts securing the rear end cover *B* and remove the cover and then the washer and the spacing shim *C*.

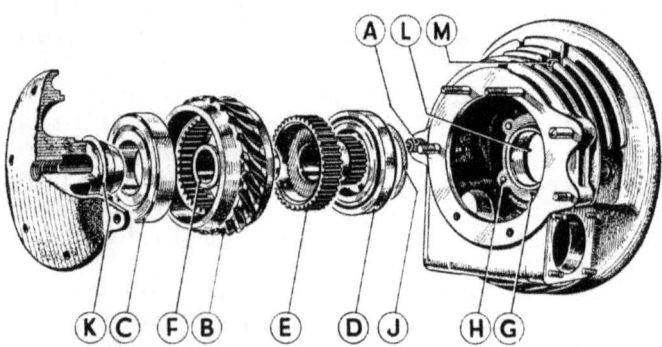

FIG. 78. FURTHER COMPONENTS OF THE REAR DRIVE
From February, 1949, the shim *J* has been omitted

Draw out the worm from the rear, applying a few taps with a soft mallet to the front end if the worm is stiff. The rear bearing housing *D*, along with the bearing, and the inner race of the front bearing *E*, will come away with the worm and can now be separated if desired. The outer part of the front bearing will stay in the front bearing housing *F*, and the housing can be

GENERAL MAINTENANCE AND OVERHAUL 115

withdrawn after removing the four securing nuts. Replace the inner race of the front bearing in its outer race, and inspect the condition of the spring-loaded oil seal G.

Referring to Fig. 78, slide out the worm wheel which will come away together with the outer race of its outer ball bearing C, the outer race of the inner bearing D, the coupling dog E, and the distance piece F. Now remove the six bolts H and detach the inner bearing carrier G and the brake gear on the outer side of the casing. Packing shims, in addition to the shim K, may be fitted between the inner bearing carrier G and the worm housing so as to position the worm wheel correctly in relation to the centre line of the worm. Finally, to effect a complete strip-down, withdraw from the worm gear casing the oil seal L, the filler plate M (secured by two screws), the brake cam from the spindle A, and the brake housing (secured by two studs).

Inspect the condition of the teeth on the worm and the worm wheel. After a very big mileage some wear may be present, and if this is excessive, you will have to fit a new worm wheel and worm shaft which can be obtained from local Sunbeam dealers or from the makers.

Assembling the Rear Drive. Reassemble the parts in the reverse order to dismantling. Little skill is required to dismantle the rear drive, but reassembly necessitates the utmost care being taken to ensure the correct alignment of the worm relatively to the worm wheel. When the wheel spindle is locked in position, the worm assembly must be truly aligned in the frame and float freely without any side thrust being present.

Wear of the shims (shown at C in Fig. 77 and J, K in Fig. 78) is most unlikely to occur and therefore you must always reassemble the identical shims formerly used. The inside of the rear cover plate has a rubber oil seal and you must be careful not to omit this seal.

Dismantling the Front Forks, Steering Head, and Rear Suspension. It is rarely necessary or advisable to strip-down these members, and considerations of space at the author's disposal do not permit of dismantling instructions being included in this chapter. For the appropriate instructions, you are therefore advised to refer to the maker's instruction manual dealing with your own particular machine.

NOTES

INDEX

ACID level, battery, 44
Alignment, headlamp, 47
Amal carburettor, 17–22
Ammeter, 7, 44
Art of Motor-cycling, 3

BAFFLE plate, cam chamber, 91
Battery, care of, 44–6
Big-end bearings, removing, 101
Bore wear, 107
Brakes—
  adjusting, 80–2
  lubricating, 40
  use of, 14
Brushes, commutator, 41–3
Bulb renewal, 48–9

CAMSHAFT—
  driving chain tension, 65
  removing, 97
Carbon deposits, removing, 89
Carburettor—
  maintenance, 26–8
  settings, 24
  tuning, 22–6
  working of, 7
Central stand, 9
Chain, timing, tension of, 65
Chromium, cleaning, 57
Circlips, gudgeon-pin, 104
Circumferential contact, ring, 105
Cleaning—
  distributor unit, 64
  machine, 56
  sparking plugs, 61–2
  sump filter, 33
Clutch—
  adjustment, 77–9
  inspecting, 113
  lever, 7
  removing, 112
Colour of exhaust, 22
Commutator, 43
  brushes, 41–3
Compensated voltage control, 43

Connecting-rods and pistons, removing, 101–3
Connexions, battery, 46
Contact-breaker—
  cam, lubricating, 33
  gap, 64
Controls, 4–9
  lubricating, 40
  setting for starting, 9
Crankshaft—
  journal wear, 101
  removal, 107–8
Cut-away throttle valve, 21, 25
Cycle parts, lubricating, 34–40
Cylinder—
  head—
    removing, 83
    replacing, 92
  liner, wear of, 107

DAMPER clearances, engine, 66
Decarbonizing, 82–92
Dip-stick, oil, 31
Dip switch, 8
Dismantling carburettor, 26
Distributor unit—
  cleaning, 64
  lubricating, 33
Downward gear changes, 12
Draining—
  gearbox, 35
  oil sump, 33
Driving licence, 2, 16
Dunlop tyre pressures, 69
Dynamo—
  lubrication, 35
  maintenance, 41–4

ELECTRIC horn, 49, 52
Electrodes, plug, re-gapping, 63
Electrolyte, battery, 44
Engine—
  and gearbox, removing, 97–9
  damper clearances, 66
  lubrication, 29
  oils, 31

Exhaust flames, 22

FILTER, sump, cleaning, 33
First gear, engaging, 11
Float chamber, 27
Flooding of carburettor, 14
Focusing headlamp, 47
Foot gear-change—
  dismantling, 110
  pedal, 7
Front—
  brake lever, 7
  forks, lubricating, 37–8
  wheel, removing, 71–3
Fuel consumption, excessive, 26

GAP—
  contact-breaker, 64
  piston ring, 106
  sparking plug, 63
Gear-change pedal, 7
Gear changing, 11–14
Gearbox—
  assembly, 111
  dismantling, 109
  draining, 35
  oil level, 35
  removal, 109
Grease gun, filling, 36
Greases, 36
Green warning light, 8
Grinding-in valves, 90–1
Gudgeon-pin, removing, 104

HEADLAMP, *Lucas*, 46
Horn—
  button, 8
  electric, 49, 52
Hub bearings, 71
Hubs, lubricating, 36

IGNITION—
  key, 6
  re-timing, 95
  suppressor sparking plugs, 60
  switch, 14
Indicator, gear-change, 7, 11
Inflation pressures, 68
Insurance, 1

JETS, carburettor, 21

KICK-STARTER—
  pedal, 6, 10
  ratchet adjustment, 79

LAMPS, 46–9, 52
Legal preliminaries, 1–3
Licences, 2
Lighting switch, 7, 46
Lights, warning, 8
Liners—
  big-end, 101
  cylinder, 107
Lubrication—
  brakes, 40
  chart, 34
  controls, 40
  distributor unit, 33
  dynamo, 35
  front forks, 37–8
  gearbox, 35
  hubs, 36
  rear suspension, 38
    universal joint, 39
  saddle suspension, 39
  speedometer drive, 40
  stands, 40
  steering head, 37

MAIN jet, 21
  size, 24
Maintenance, items for, 53
Major overhaul, 96–115
Marking pistons, 104
Mixture—
  rich, 23
  weak, 22
Moving off, 11

NEEDLE—
  jet, 21, 28
  position, 25
  tapered, 21
Neutral, 9
Nuts, tightness of, 57

OBSTRUCTION, pilot jet, 26
Oil—
  circulation, 29
  level, sump, 30
  pump, 107
Oils, engine, 31

INDEX

Overhead—
  camshaft, removing, 97
  rocker assembly, dismantling, 96
  rockers, removing, 87

PETROL taps, 4
Pillion riding, 2
Pilot—
  air-adjusting screw, 21
  jet—
    adjusting, 25
    obstruction, 26
Piston—
  ring gap, 106
  rings—
    inspecting, 105
    removing, 104
  seizure, 15
Pistons and connecting-rods, removing, 101–3
Pistons, removing, 103–4
Pitted valves, 90
Plug—
  gap, 63
  trouble, 60
  types, 59
Pressure—
  oil, 32
  tyre, 68
Prop stand, 9
Pump—
  driving gear, 33
  oil, 32

RATCHET adjustment, kick-starter, 79
Rear—
  brake pedal, 7, 82
  drive, dismantling, 113
  suspension, lubricating, 38
  wheel, removing, 71–3
Red reflectors, 52
Red warning light, 8
Repairs, 53, 56
Rich mixture, 23
Rings, piston, removing, 104
Running-in, 15

SADDLE—
  adjustment, 70
  suspension, 39

Segments, commutator, 43
Seizure, piston, 15
Service tools, 55
Sidecar—
  single-seater, 4
  toe-in, 70
Slow-running, bad, 26
Spares, 53
Sparking plugs, suitable, 59
Specific gravity, battery, 45–6
Speedometer—
  drive—
    detaching, 111
    lubricating, 40
  law regarding, 2
Springs, valve, 91
Stands—
  lubricating, 40
  use of, 9
Starting procedure, 9–11
Steering—
  damper, 8
  head—
    adjustment, 73–6
    lubrication, 37, 40
Stop-tail lamp, 48
Stopping, 14
Strangler, carburettor, 6, 10
Sump—
  draining, 33
  filter, cleaning, 33
  oil level, 30
Sunbeam controls, 4–9
Switch—
  dip, 8
  ignition, 6, 14
  lighting, 7, 46

THROTTLE—
  stop, 6
  stop screw, 20
  twist-grip, 6
  valve cut-away, 21, 25
Timing—
  chain tension, 65
  gears, dismantling, 107
  ignition, 95
  valves, 92
Toe-in, sidecar, 70
Tool kit, 55
Topping-up battery, 44
Tray, filter, 33

Twin-gear oil pump, 32
Twist-grip, 6
Tyre maintenance, 68

UNIVERSAL joint, rear, lubricating, 39
Upper cylinder lubricant, 16
Upward gear changes, 12

VALVE—
 clearances, 57–9
 spring removal, 91
Valves—
 assembling, 91
 grinding-in, 90

Valves (*contd.*)—
 removing, 87
 retiming, 92
Vandervell big-end liners, 101
Voltage control, 43

WARMING-UP engine, 11
Warning lights, 8, 48
Watertight sparking plugs, 59
Weak mixture, 22
Weatherproof plug terminal covers, 59
Wet sump lubrication system, 29
Wheel bearings, 71
Wiring diagrams, 50, 51
Worm drive lubrication, 35

AUTOBOOKS WORKSHOP MANUALS

ALFA ROMEO GIULIA 1300, 1600, 1750, 2000 1962-1978 WSM
BMW 1600 1966-1973 WSM
BMW 2000 & 2002 1966-1976 WSM
BMW 2500, 2800, 3.0 & 3.3 1968-1977 WSM
BMW 316, 320, 320i 1975-1977 WSM
BMW 518, 520, 520i 1973-1981 WSM
FIAT 1100, 1100D, 1100R & 1200 1957-1969 WSM
FIAT 124 1966-1974 WSM
FIAT 124 SPORT 1966-1975 WSM
FIAT 125 & 125 SPECIAL 1967-1973 WSM
FIAT 126, 126L, 126 DV, 126/650 & 126/650 DV 1972-1982 WSM
FIAT 127 SALOON, SPECIAL & SPORT, 900, 1050 1971-1981 WSM
FIAT 128 1969-1982 WSM
FIAT 1300, 1500 1961-1967 WSM
FIAT 131 MIRAFIORI 1975-1982 WSM
FIAT 132 1972-1982 WSM
FIAT 500 1957-1973 WSM
FIAT 600, 600D & MULTIPLA 1955-1969 WSM
FIAT 850 1964-1972 WSM
JAGUAR E-TYPE 1961-1972 WSM
JAGUAR MK 1, 2 1955-1969 WSM
JAGUAR S TYPE, 420 1963-1968 WSM
JAGUAR XK 120, 140, 150 MK 7, 8, 9 1948-1961 WSM
LAND ROVER 1, 2 1948-1961 WSM
MERCEDES-BENZ 190 1959-1968 WSM
MERCEDES-BENZ 220/8 1968-1972 WSM
MERCEDES-BENZ 220B 1959-1965 WSM
MERCEDES-BENZ 230 1963-1968 WSM
MERCEDES-BENZ 250 1968-1972 WSM
MERCEDES-BENZ 280 1968-1972 WSM
MG MIDGET TA-TF 1936-1955 WSM
MINI 1959-1980 WSM
MORRIS MINOR 1952-1971 WSM
PEUGEOT 404 1960-1975 WSM
PORSCHE 911 1964-1973 WSM
PORSCHE 911 1970-1977 WSM
RENAULT 16 1965-1979 WSM
RENAULT 8, 10, 1100 1962-1971 WSM
ROVER 3500, 3500S 1968-1976 WSM
SUNBEAM RAPIER, ALPINE 1955-1965 WSM
TRIUMPH SPITFIRE, GT6, VITESSE 1962-1968 WSM
TRIUMPH TR2, TR3, TR3A 1952-1962 WSM
TRIUMPH TR4, TR4A 1961-1967 WSM
VOLKSWAGEN BEETLE 1968-1977 WSM

VELOCEPRESS AUTOMOBILE BOOKS & MANUALS

ABARTH BUYERS GUIDE
AUSTIN-HEALEY 6-CYLINDER WSM
AUSTIN-HEALEY SPRITE & MG MIDGET 1958-1971 WSM
BMW 600 LIMOUSINE FACTORY WSM
BMW 600 LIMOUSINE OWNERS HAND BOOK & SERVICE MANUAL
BMW ISETTA FACTORY WSM
BOOK OF THE CARRERA PANAMERICANA - MEXICAN ROAD RACE
COMPLETE CATALOG OF JAPANESE MOTOR VEHICLES
CORVAIR 1960-1969 OWNERS WORKSHOP MANUAL
CORVETTE V8 1955-1962 OWNERS WORKSHOP MANUAL
DIALED IN - THE JAN OPPERMAN STORY
FERRARI 250/GT SERVICE AND MAINTENANCE
FERRARI 308 SERIES BUYER'S AND OWNER'S GUIDE
FERRARI BERLINETTA LUSSO
FERRARI BROCHURES AND SALES LITERATURE 1946-1967
FERRARI BROCHURES AND SALES LITERATURE 1968-1989
FERRARI GUIDE TO PERFORMANCE
FERRARI OPP, MAINTENANCE & SERVICE H/BOOKS 1948-1963
FERRARI OWNER'S HANDBOOK
FERRARI SERIAL NUMBERS PART I - ODD NUMBERS TO 21399
FERRARI SERIAL NUMBERS PART II - EVEN NUMBERS TO 1050
FERRARI SPYDER CALIFORNIA
FERRARI TUNING TIPS & MAINTENANCE TECHNIQUES
HENRY'S FABULOUS MODEL "A" FORD
HOW TO BUILD A FIBERGLASS CAR
HOW TO BUILD A RACING CAR
HOW TO RESTORE THE MODEL 'A' FORD
IF HEMINGWAY HAD WRITTEN A RACING NOVEL
JAGUAR E-TYPE 3.8 & 4.2 WSM
LE MANS 24 (THE BOOK THAT THE FILM WAS BASED ON)
MASERATI BROCHURES AND SALES LITERATURE
MASERATI OWNER'S HANDBOOK
METROPOLITAN FACTORY WSM
MGA & MGB OWNERS HANDBOOK & WSM
OBERT'S FIAT GUIDE
PERFORMANCE TUNING THE SUNBEAM TIGER
PORSCHE 356 1948-1965 WSM
PORSCHE 912 WSM
SOUPING THE VOLKSWAGEN
TRIUMPH TR2, TR3, TR4 1953-1965 WSM
TUNING FOR SPEED (P.E. IRVING)
VEDA ORR'S NEW REVISED HOT ROD PICTORIAL
VOLKSWAGEN TRANSPORTER, TRUCKS, STATION WAGONS WSM
VOLVO 1944-1968 ALL MODELS WSM
WEBER CARBURETORS (EMPHASIS ON ALFA & FIAT)

BROOKLANDS BOOKS & ROAD TEST PORTFOLIOS (RTP)

AC CARS 1904-2009
ALFA ROMEO 1920-1933 ROAD TEST PORTFOLIO
ALFA ROMEO 1934-1940 ROAD TEST PORTFOLIO
BRABHAM RALT HONDA THE RON TAURANAC STORY
BUGATTI TYPE 10 TO TYPE 40 ROAD TEST PORTFOLIO
BUGATTI TYPE 10 TO TYPE 251 ROAD TEST PORTFOLIO
BUGATTI TYPE 41 TO TYPE 55 ROAD TEST PORTFOLIO
BUGATTI TYPE 57 TO TYPE 251 ROAD TEST PORTFOLIO
DELAHAYE ROAD TEST PORTFOLIO
FERRARI ROAD CARS 1946-1956 ROAD TEST PORTFOLIO
FIAT 500 1936-1972 ROAD TEST PORTFOLIO
FIAT DINO ROAD TEST PORTFOLIO
HISPANO SUIZA ROAD TEST PORTFOLIO
HONDA ST1100/ST1300 PAN EUROPEAN 1990-2002 RTP
JAGUAR MK1 & MK2 ROAD TEST PORTFOLIO
LOTUS CORTINA ROAD TEST PORTFOLIO
MV AGUSTA F4 750 & 1000 1997-2007 ROAD TEST PORTFOLIO
TATRA CARS ROAD TEST PORTFOLIO

VELOCEPRESS MOTORCYCLE BOOKS & MANUALS

AJS SINGLES & TWINS 250cc THRU 1000cc 1932-1948 (BOOK OF)
AJS SINGLES 1955-65 350cc & 500cc (BOOK OF)
AJS SINGLES 1945-60 350cc & 500cc MODELS 16 & 18 (BOOK OF)
ARIEL 1939-1960 4 STROKE SINGLES (BOOK OF)
ARIEL LEADER & ARROW 1958-1964 (BOOK OF)
ARIEL MOTORCYCLES 1933-1951 WSM
ARIEL PREWAR MODELS 1932-1939 (BOOK OF)
BMW M/CYCLES R26 R27 (1956-1967) FACTORY WSM
BMW M/CYCLES R50 R50S R60 R69S (1955-1969) FACTORY WSM
BSA BANTAM (BOOK OF)
BSA ALL FOUR-STROKE SINGLES & V-TWINS 1936-1952 (BOOK OF)
BSA OHV & SV SINGLES - 250cc 1954-1970 (BOOK OF)
BSA OHV & SV SINGLES 1945-54 250-600cc (BOOK OF)
BSA OHV SINGLES 350 & 500cc 1955-1967 (BOOK OF)
BSA PRE-WAR MODELS TO 1939 (BOOK OF)
BSA TWINS 1948-1962 (BOOK OF)
BSA TWINS 1962-1969 (SECOND BOOK OF)
CATALOG OF BRITISH MOTORCYCLES (1951 MODELS)
DOUGLAS PRE-WAR ALL MODELS 1929-1939 (BOOK OF)
DOUGLAS POST-WAR ALL MODELS 1948-1957 FACTORY WSM
DUCATI 160cc, 250cc & 350cc OHC MODELS FACTORY WSM
HONDA 50 ALL MODELS UP TO 1970 INC MONKEY & TRAIL (BOOK OF)
HONDA 90 ALL MODELS UP TO 1966 (BOOK OF)
HONDA MOTORCYCLES 125-150 TWINS C/CS/CB/CA WSM
HONDA MOTORCYCLES 250-305 TWINS C/CS/CB WSM
HONDA MOTORCYCLES C100 SUPER CUB WSM
HONDA MOTORCYCLES C110 SPORT CUB 1962-1969 WSM
HONDA TWINS & SINGLES 50cc THRU 305cc 1960-1966 (BOOK OF)
HONDA TWINS ALL MODELS 125cc THRU 450cc UP TO 1968 (BOOK OF)
INDIAN PONYBIKE, BOY RACER & PAPOOSE ILL PARTS LIST & SALES LIT
LAMBRETTA ALL 125 & 150cc MODELS 1947-1957 (BOOK OF)
LAMBRETTA LI & TV MODELS 1957-1970 (SECOND BOOK OF)
MATCHLESS 350 & 500cc SINGLES 1945-1956 (BOOK OF)
MATCHLESS 350 & 500cc SINGLES 1955-1966 (BOOK OF)
NORTON 1932-1947 (BOOK OF)
NORTON 1938-1956 (BOOK OF)
NORTON DOMINATOR TWINS 1955-1965 (BOOK OF)
NORTON MODELS 19, 50 & ES2 1955-1963 (BOOK OF)
NORTON MOTORCYCLES 1957-1970 FACTORY WSM
NORTON PREWAR MODELS 1932-1939 (BOOK OF)
NSU QUICKLY ALL MODELS 1953-1963 (BOOK OF)
ROYAL ENFIELD SINGLES & V TWINS 1937-1953 (BOOK OF)
ROYAL ENFIELD SINGLES 1946-1962 (BOOK OF)
ROYAL ENFIELD 736cc INTERCEPTOR FACTORY WSM
ROYAL ENFIELD 250cc & 350cc SINGLES 1958-1966 (SECOND BOOK OF)
SUNBEAM S7 & S8 (BOOK OF)
SUZUKI 50cc & 80cc UP TO 1966 (BOOK OF)
SUZUKI T10 1963-1967 FACTORY WSM
SUZUKI T20 & T200 1965-1969 FACTORY WSM
TRIUMPH PRE-WAR MOTORCYCLE 1935-1939 (BOOK OF)
TRIUMPH MOTORCYCLES 1937-1951 WSM
TRIUMPH MOTORCYCLES 1945-1955 FACTORY WSM
TRIUMPH TWINS 1956-1969 (BOOK OF)
VELOCETTE ALL SINGLES & TWINS 1925-1970 (BOOK OF)
VESPA 1951-1961 (BOOK OF)
VESPA 125 & 150cc & GS MODELS 1955-1963 (SECOND BOOK OF)
VESPA 90, 125 & 150cc 1963-1972 (THIRD BOOK OF)
VESPA GS & SS 1955-1968 (BOOK OF)
VILLIERS ENGINE (BOOK OF)
VINCENT MOTORCYCLES 1935-1955 WSM

PLEASE VISIT OUR WEBSITE
www.VelocePress.com
FOR A DETAILED DESCRIPTION
OF ANY OF THESE TITLES

Please check our website:

www.VelocePress.com

for a complete
up-to-date list of
available titles

www.ingramcontent.com/pod-product-compliance
Lightning Source LLC
Chambersburg PA
CBHW070555170426
43201CB00012B/1849